INSTRUCTIONS NOT SUPPLIED

A STORY OF ADOPTION, AUTISM AND COMING TOGETHER AS A FAMILY

Julie Otto

First published in Great Britain by Practical Inspiration Publishing, 2018

© Julie Otto, 2018

The moral rights of the author have been asserted

ISBN 978-1-788-60025-5

Practical Inspiration
PUBLISHING

To my husband Steve
and our boys,
Connor, Stephen and Harry

CONTENTS

ACKNOWLEDGEMENTS

Tradition states that the author thanks those people who have contributed to the writing of a book. This book is all about us and our family, it seems not enough to simply list them in a few short paragraphs. But here goes.

Firstly Steve, my husband and my best friend. We have been through a great deal so far and I am sure there are plenty more challenges to come. We both had no idea what was in front of us when we embarked on having a family, but we are here, and we remain strong.

To my mum, Granny, Pauline Wade. She has been there throughout. She has watched from a distance and been there when we needed her. She loves her grandchildren unconditionally and they love her.

And to our boys, Connor, Stephen and Harry. You have changed our lives and given us so much joy. As you all grow into adulthood, you will know that you are loved and cherished and for every moment, for every challenge along the way, we will get there.

FOREWORD

"A good heart is better than all the heads in the world."
    Edward George Earle Lytton Bulwer-Lytton (1803–1873)

I TRAINED AS a clinical psychologist at the Institute of Psychiatry in London. During my training, together with some of my classmates, I worked with a charity in Camden that specialised in working with families who had adopted "difficult to place" children. We provided support to a range of families and individuals who had adopted children who were either past the "cute" stage and older than most families were looking to adopt, or who had additional needs, such as autism, ADHD or Down syndrome. I greatly admired these families who had taken on children they knew had additional issues and who were committed to giving them a warm and accepting family, come what may.

More recently, I have run groups for emergency foster parents, who often have to take on children with major neurodevelopment and behavioural issues at short notice and without preparation.

I have known Julie Otto, her family (husband Steve and their three sons, Connor, Stephen and Harry), her many pets (dogs, cats and tortoises) and her boundless enthusiasm for a number of years. I was more than happy to agree when she approached me to write a foreword for her first book. Julie seems to have endless energy and I am as likely to bump into her giving golf lessons or running her dogs on the beach with the boys as discussing autistic spectrum disorder (ASD) with her.

When I saw the title Julie had decided on for their book, *Instructions Not Supplied*, my thoughts went back to Christmases when my own girls were small and Ros and I would busily wrap presents once we knew the girls were sound asleep. There always seemed to be large must-have presents that needed to be wrapped and put under the tree for Christmas morning. Almost inevitably, at least one box would have a small label somewhere that we had overlooked when shopping that said "Batteries not included". Discovering this was usually followed by a frantic but fruitless search through drawers for the three AAA and six C batteries Santa would need to acquire at the last minute. Asking the obvious question when we had bought the game/toy/laptop in the first place would have made Christmases easier to plan.

No child, whether adopted, fostered or brought up in their biological family, comes supplied with an instruction booklet or an information leaflet on what to ask about or with suggestions as to what additional inputs are available locally or might be required. The lists of instructions and questions would be different for any child, and thinking about the more predictable questions you might need to be prepared for is the best approach. There are no instructions, but you are holding a brief book that gives you an excellent start on developing what you need.

When Julie and Steve adopted Connor at 21 months, his delayed language, stereotyped motor patterns and attachment issues were fairly obvious but were put down to the effects of his poor early care.

Connor and Harry are biological brothers and both had been placed in care from birth. Harry had an inguinal hernia which had not been treated, and Julie gives a fairly graphic account of an emergency visit to the Royal Hospital for Sick Children in Edinburgh when he required surgery to correct this.

Their (biologically unrelated) brother Stephen had been taken into care at 51 weeks of age due to parental neglect. He was born with part of his bowel outside his body (gastroschisis) and has only one functioning kidney. Stephen was slower to develop than Connor, but again this was thought to have been due to his difficult early first year.

I am sure that many people reading this will come across themes common to families coping with unexpected issues and wondering about a possible ASD diagnosis. The journey the Ottos have been on, the various questions they have had to ask and the hurdles they have found blocking their road at different stages will be helpful to many in asking the right questions, challenging decisions and planning ahead. The results of planning, perseverance and developing an understanding of how the various systems involved can work (and can also clash) are clearly shown in Julie's descriptions, and the positive loving family that the Ottos have built for their boys is plain for all to see.

Instructions Not Supplied is a readable, positive book with a clear message: adoption can be rewarding, and children should be treated as individuals, not as bundles of issues diagnoses. Julie, Steve, Connor, Stephen and

Harry should be an inspiration to those who struggle with many of the issues described here.

"It is the lives we encounter that make life worth living."

Guy de Maupassant
(1850–1893)

Dr Ken Aitken
Senior Lecturer, Institute of Health and Wellness,
University of Glasgow
Researcher, The Rivers Centre, Edinburgh
External Lecturer, University of Birmingham
External Associate, University of São Paulo
Ad hoc Adviser on autism to the Scottish Minister for
Health

INTRODUCTION

IT'S JANUARY 2005, the day after the Christmas break from work, and Steve and I sit in his office in St Andrews. Steve picks up the phone and makes the call that will change the rest of our lives together. It is a phone call to our local authority's adoption and fostering service asking about the procedure to adopt a child.

A phone call like that does not come out of the blue, it comes after a great deal of consideration, thought, discussion and an overwhelming desire to have a family. We were married in 2003; in fact, Steve proposed on the Saturday night of the 2002 Open Championship in our hotel room a few miles from Muirfield golf club. I was too tired to hear what he was saying as it had been a hectic couple of weeks of work, so he had to repeat the question. Having said that, it was all rather romantic – he had bought a painting that we had seen in North Berwick the previous week, and both just loved. It still hangs in our study at home. He showed me the painting rather proudly and then said a few things that I was meant to understand. Now, I had been up at 4am to drive to Muirfield, first on site that morning to take tee markers out, check and set up the course for the third day of the 2002 Open. It was the day of many seasons that saw Tiger Woods scoring in the 80s and players hiding behind advertising boards to shelter from the inclement weather. It had been a long day, so hardly surprising that I did not work out where this painting was taking the conversation.

We were married in St Andrews the following year. Both married before but with no children from previous relationships, we hoped to be able to start a family and enjoy a "normal" life. To be fair, I am not sure what a normal life is. However, it became evident that we were not able to conceive. After much discussion, including a referral for further investigation from our GP, over the Christmas break of 2004 we made the decision that the assisted conception route was not one we wanted to follow. We discussed in depth the pros and cons of adopting as we understood them at that time, and we decided that we would make the call to start the process.

Now this book is not an autobiography; there are certainly parts of my life that only my family and closest of friends will be part of. This book is written to share some of the experiences of an aspect of our lives together; looking at the process that we went through to adopt our boys and the difficulties we have and are encountering since. It is not a complete history of that period – there are parts of the process and challenges that we faced that must remain confidential to protect our children. But all the situations and examples are a true account of our lives. We are now parents of three boys, all adopted, and all with various degrees of disability and difficulty. In January 2005 we had no idea where that phone call would take us and even less idea of the difficulties that we would encounter along the way.

The process to adopt children is a lengthy one, which is probably not a surprise to most of you reading this. It is traumatic, drawn out and extremely emotional for any prospective adopter. It is not a process that should be undertaken lightly. I should say at this point that we have three wonderful boys who are one hundred per cent our children and we love them all dearly.

The reason for putting pen to paper, or rather opening a Word document and starting to type, is to offer a unique insight into the twin challenges of adoption and disability; to share some of the issues and difficulties that we experienced during the adoption process, and to talk about the problems we have and are now encountering in parenting children with disabilities and difficulties. Our boys have a range of problems, some directly linked to adoption, but most are either genetic or just them and their own make-up. Asperger's syndrome and autism (both autistic spectrum disorders), attention deficit hyperactivity disorder (usually referred to as ADHD), foetal alcohol syndrome (FAS), learning disabilities, anxiety behaviours and attachment disorder, the difficulties associated with these conditions we face on a day-to-day basis.

As diagnosis techniques for conditions such as those our children suffer from improve, more and more families find themselves parenting children with a "diagnosis". I hope that this account of our experiences both in adopting and in dealing with disabilities and difficulties can help and support other adoptive parents and prospective adopters, as well as natural parents of children with special educational needs. For teachers and medical practitioners, I hope to give an insight into family life of parenting such children and the type of support that might have been helpful to us and to other families facing similar challenges. Education is the key to success, but that is not just the education of the child. It is equipping the adults that support them on both a personal and a professional level with the knowledge to do so effectively.

Who we are

With any book that is effectively about the author and the people around them, it is probably a good start to tell you a little about who I am and who we are.

My name is Julie Otto and together with my husband, Steve, this is about us and our family, and of course how we all came to be together. I was born in Suffolk and lived there until the age of 29, when I moved to Scotland. Leaving school at 16 years old I went to work for an insurance company while I maintained my love of playing golf. Between the ages of 19 and 29 I represented both England and Great Britain and Ireland in international golf competitions and won a total of 14 national titles. My father had encouraged me at a young age to play golf and he revelled in my success. He would have been a wonderful grandfather, but sadly he died of cancer at the rather young age of 63 and before I met Steve. I retired from competitive golf at the age of 29, taking up a position in golf administration, first with the Ladies' Golf Union and then with The Royal and Ancient Golf Club of St Andrews (The R&A). I travelled the world both playing and working in the game that I loved. Latterly, and after we had adopted our boys, I turned my hand to professional golf, mostly in a coaching capacity while mentoring assistant professionals through the Professional Golfers' Association training programme. I am often asked why I decided to go into golf coaching – the answer will become evident as you read through this book.

Steve was born in Poole in Dorset and discovered at a young age a love of mathematics. He has a first-class honours degree, a PhD from Exeter University and worked for NASA as a staff scientist for a few years after his degrees. Returning from the United States he took up a lecturing position at the University of Birmingham, where one of his outside contracts saw him working as a consultant with The R&A. There, two very different worlds collided. Steve left academia just after we married and took up a permanent position with The R&A, where he still works.

A brief overview of where we come from, who we are now, is probably very different from who we were when we met in 2001. Experiences in life change us, everyone has a past, and you simply cannot get to where you are without one. It is the future that is important, and getting through the next few years with teenage boys may be more of a challenge than parenting "normal" kids. Ah, that word "normal". One thing I have learned over the past few years is that there is no such thing. A lovely phrase that I picked up is "neuro-typical", defined by *The Oxford English Dictionary* as "not displaying or characterised by autistic or other neurologically atypical patterns of thought or behaviour". Our children are not neuro-typical, all three have an autistic spectrum diagnosis and all three are very different people, just like all of us neuro-typical people are different. While there are clearly some very talented autistic people in the world, it is a huge mistake to watch the film *Rain Man*, with Dustin Hoffman playing a talented autistic savant, and assume that all people with autism are "clever" in some way. We all have things we are better at than others and in our experience that is the case in either the neuro-typical or the autistic world. For us, such a huge part of who we are now is being moulded by gaining a greater understanding of the people around us.

There you have it, we are the parents in this story, Julie and Steve. Our children are Connor, Stephen and Harry, and we live in Fife with our four dogs, two cats and two tortoises.

Chapter 1

HOW IT ALL BEGAN

Adoption – preparing for a child the adoptive way

I would imagine that the majority of people who would like to become parents prepare in some way before embarking on such a massive change in their lives. We certainly did, we just did not know at that time that having a family naturally would be something that was not open to us. From the moment of conception to giving birth there is time to adjust to the prospect of a baby entering your world and what changes that will bring. In this first chapter, I share some of the experiences we had going through the adoption process, from the time of first contact with the adoption agency to completing our family.

After that life-changing phone call in January 2005, a social worker arrived at our house the very next evening to make an initial contact and start the process. The first stage was to attend a "preparation course" and we were advised that luckily one was starting the following week and there was space for us to attend if we would like to take things forward. It was all quite overwhelming but exciting at the same time.

Off we went into our first meeting of the preparation course, a group meeting with seven couples in the room – six heterosexual couples, one-same sex couple and a single lady who wanted to adopt from Guatemala. We all sat in a circle and then came the dreaded introducing yourself and saying why you wanted to adopt. Steve wanted to get up and introduce us with a quip that would probably have been marked down as inappropriate, but he behaved himself and spoke in his ever confident and professional manner. Compared with the rest of the process, the preparation course was probably the least intrusive. I still remember that day when everyone stood in turn and came up with pretty much the same reason: because they could not have a family naturally.

I am not sure how many weeks we attended the course – I think there were six or eight sessions in total, usually in the evenings – but the final day was a full day of instruction. If I could turn back the clock, there are many questions I would have asked. The social workers delivering the course gave an outline of many aspects of the process and the types of children that find themselves, through no fault of their own, in the care system today. They attempted to give an insight into the types of behaviour that can result from early years of neglect or abuse. If I am to be very honest, Steve and I sat and listened to the discussion believing that any child placed with us would not present in such a manner. How wrong we were.

It is our experience, and the experience of many adoptive parents, that our children have some problems that either come from a troubled early life or are genetically based. It is that question of nature versus nurture and which aspect provides the more significant contribution.

Our children all have accents and mannerisms that they have picked up from simply being our boys. Yet some of their difficulties arise from neglect and abuse either before birth (for example, foetal alcohol syndrome) or after birth (for example, neglect of basic level of care). Some are possibly genetically based, such as our second son's learning disability or being autistic, which is one for the more qualified clinicians among you.

The preparation course did cover these things but presented them in such a dramatic fashion that we simply thought they could not apply to all children and there must be some "normal" ones among them. There is that word again. I remember us sitting around in a semi-circle listening to the social worker as she went through slides on the effects of FAS and the physical characteristics of that condition. The images she showed us were dramatic and heart-wrenching, but still it was like a story or documentary that would affect others and not us.

A few sessions into the preparation course, we started to tell our family and friends what we were doing. They were all supportive, and as this knowledge spread wider, numerous people that we came across or whom we had been close to confided in us that they were adopted. One such person was Jennie Rigg, a wonderful lady and wife of the then chief medical officer to The R&A for the Open Championship. I remember quite vividly working at the Royal Liverpool Golf Club for the 2006 Open and Jennie coming bounding across the tented village to speak to me. She was so enthusiastic. She herself was an adopted child and for her, adoption was the best thing that had ever happened in her life. This further embedded in our minds the fact that it was unlikely that children placed with us would have any significant issues. Of course, the people we were talking to were adults, placed for adoption as babies at a time when it was socially unacceptable to have a child outside marriage. In fact, one of my closest colleagues at the time had spoken of when his (adoptive) mother had told him about being handed her baby on a pavement in London outside the adoption agency offices near Harrods. Today, of course, things are somewhat different. Many of the children in the care system that will eventually be placed for adoption are from very different backgrounds and are often in care for their own safety.

The one area that was not well covered in the preparation course was the legal aspect. During our time in the adoption process, which started in January 2005 and finished when we legally adopted our third child in December 2009, we attended or were represented at numerous panel meetings and hearings. Starting under one legal system for our first two children, the system changed mid-way through the process to adopt our third child. Interestingly, all three seemed to proceed on a different track – hearings for one did not occur in another's case and so on. It was complicated and difficult to follow, something that should have been covered in greater detail as we embarked on what would be a lengthy and emotional experience. I should say, for clarification, that this adoption process was under Scottish law and a completely different system would apply outside Scotland.

Other than the obvious and perhaps not so obvious issues with adoption, the "preparation phase" of thinking about the future with a family is probably not too dissimilar to that of couples who conceive and have a child naturally: the expectation of the arrival of a baby or child into our lives, what impact that would have on our careers and our lives in general; the excitement of what was ahead; of course, all the purchases that needed to be made, decorating a room, buying the necessary equipment. The main difference was that our child would not be a newborn; he or she would already have had some life experience and most likely would have been placed with foster carers. The age of the child was simply unknown. Generally, I think the younger the better for adoption, but having said that, there are significant numbers of children in the care system who would relish the opportunity of a new "forever" family. Our boys were 21 months, 2 years and 3 months and 11 months old when placed for adoption with us. Two were in care from birth for their own safety. Our middle son, however, had suffered in his short life, being taken into care a week short of his first birthday, unable to move his arms and legs through the neglect that he had suffered. More of this later, and certainly lessons to be learned from his experience and the experience of the people picking up the pieces of such a situation.

Being assessed

So there we were, through the preparation course and now embarking on the lengthy interviews and checking process that would occur constantly over the next few months.

For us, the assessment process took approximately seven months from the time of our initial enquiry and application to being approved by an adoption panel as prospective adopters. For some of you reading this, that may sound like an awfully long time, but there were some couples on our initial preparation course that were not presented to the adoption panel for a much longer period. In fact, a couple that we met on the preparation course and are still friends with today were in the assessment process for ten months before approval.

It does seem like a very long time ago now, but thinking back there were numerous visits to our house by the two social workers appointed to assess our case. Steve and I met when we were both 34 years old, so we had some catching up to do. From the start of our relationship we had always been open with each other. One of our favourite discussions over dinner was to tell each other something personal that the other did not know. From childhood experiences to work or previous relationships, basically we know each other very well indeed. Strangely, this was hugely beneficial during the assessment process – nothing one of us said to social workers was a surprise to the other, and we could have easily answered for each other as the questions became more and more probing. At the end of the period they probably knew just as much as we did about ourselves.

It was a difficult time, the thought that these two people, visiting our house, gaining references and information from our friends and family, were constantly judging us, our pasts and our reasons for wanting to adopt a child. It was without doubt an emotional rollercoaster. Even our vet had to provide a reference to say that our pets were well cared for. Throughout the process we felt unnecessarily "tested" at times. For instance, in preparation for our case to be presented to an adoption panel, paperwork had to be submitted in advance. This information was referred to as "Form F". Containing all the information that had been collated by the social workers, this form included references and statements from others, information on our past, where we came from, medical history and current medical information. Above all, it included the social workers' recommendations. Aware that we would be asked to review its content prior to its submission, we asked at quite an early stage for a certain time in our diary to be avoided. It was the 2005 Open Championship at St Andrews. Both of us were working for The R&A, starting at 5 a.m. and not finishing until 10–11 p.m. on Championship days. We were presented with the paperwork in the middle of the very week we had asked to be kept clear, and were given 24 hours to review the form and provide any feedback or comments. It just felt like it was another aspect of the test of suitability.

The forms and information were submitted and a date set for the adoption panel hearing to decide whether we would be suitable to adopt a child. I remember sitting outside the room while the social workers went in to present our case. The time seemed to go very slowly indeed; we were told to expect a wait while the case was presented and that the social workers would be asked many questions on the report submitted. It took around 20 minutes and then the door opened and one of the social workers had a beaming smile of good news.

It was such a relief. The process of assessment became an emotional rollercoaster. Even though we were both working, which was certainly the best thing to do during this time, our thoughts and discussions constantly dwelled on the process we were going through.

Unbeknown to us, the tough times were to follow.

Considering and having a child

After we were approved as adoptive parents came the long wait for a match with a child. The social workers told us that following approval we would not be contacted for at least two months to allow us time to get used to the idea of having a family. To this day I struggle to understand why this was the case. The previous seven months of assessments and the months before making the phone call to the adoption and fostering service were certainly not without considering the idea of having a family.

What felt like an already lengthy process had only just begun. It was a little over nine months before the social worker called to ask whether she could come to see us to discuss a possible match. Excited was an understatement.

I previously mentioned that all our details were submitted to the adoption panel on a "Form F"; well, a child's information is also contained in a special document, referred to, at that time, as a "Form E". During the process to be approved as adoptive parents we understood that when the time came we would be shown this document on a confidential basis to consider the facts. However, what happened was almost comical. The social worker sat in an armchair in our living room and read out extracts of the document but would not let us read it ourselves. This was on Good Friday in April 2006. Having heard this information, we were asked to consider the facts and then come back with our thoughts after the Easter weekend. We were told not to discuss the matter with anyone, including our family. How crazy this all seems now. In taking in the details of this child that would become our son, it would have been so beneficial to speak to someone we trusted to gain that independent and impartial view of the facts of the case, as simple or as complicated as those facts might have been.

So a sleepless Easter break, spent on our own so we didn't spill the beans to anyone that we had been approached. As you read this I am sure you will realise that come the Tuesday after Easter, we contacted the social worker and said "yes" to the proposed match. Again, we were told not to tell anyone, she would come back to us in due course. Time seemed to move very slowly from this point. Our son was then just over 18 months old and it would be another three and a half months before we would meet him. We decided at some point during this period that we would share our good news with our friends and family, and we had a duty to our employers to advise them, as would be the case if we were expecting a child naturally. Again, this is one of those situations where it is difficult to see where the social workers were coming from in their advice and request not to share our news. Surely, like natural parents, we should decide when we felt the time was appropriate to tell our family and our friends that we would be having a son. Which, of course, we did.

So here we were, the adoption panel hearing to formally match us with Connor had taken place and a date was set for introductions to start. We had both been working at The Open at Royal Liverpool Golf Club that week. We left as Tiger Woods hit his second shot into the 18th green; there was no doubt that he would become the Open Champion. We drove up through the night to prepare for the next day and the next chapter in our lives. It was 1 p.m. on a sunny Monday afternoon that we met a little boy in a red hat, standing at the gate of a small house in Cowdenbeath in Fife.

Connor had been in foster care since birth. He had been the subject of a child protection order for his safety and was very well attached to his foster carer. She was an elderly lady who had fostered more than one hundred children in her career. Shortly after Connor was placed with us, she was awarded an MBE from the Queen for her services to foster care.

There we were in her house with Connor, our son. He was non-verbal at 21 months old, his only attempt at words was to look at any vehicle going past and say "Ca Ca". To be honest, we did not know whether this was "normal" or whether, looking back, it was a sign of what was to follow. He clearly liked repeated actions. I remember that first day in the lady's small back yard playing with Connor. There was an umbrella on the outside table and he wanted it spun round and round continuously. He then walked, or toddled, up and down the back steps of the house with joy on his face every time he reached the top or the bottom. For the clinicians or behavioural experts reading this, I can see you all smiling and nodding to yourselves, yes, certainly behaviour that would suggest something other than "neuro-typical".

We had met the foster carer before that day when she had come to visit us at our house. She was wonderful at telling us all about Connor, his likes, his dislikes and his personality. She was an accomplished foster carer, clearly preparing children for their futures, and was a godsend at teaching us the basics, including nappy changing. For all of you who have had children from birth or perhaps adopted at a very young age, you will have missed out on the experience of your child running off in the middle of your first attempt at a nappy change. She understood Connor and just knew how well he would make the move to his permanent home. She was adamant that the introductions should not take too long and from the outset she did everything in her power to help us. For this we are forever thankful.

Cowdenbeath is probably more famous for its politician, Prime Minister Gordon Brown, than anything else. Just under the hour from our house, each day for seven days we travelled to and from the foster carer's house to spend time with our son. It was certainly a tiring and emotional week. Thankfully, this accomplished foster carer was extremely supportive and at the meeting on the eighth day to decide a plan to move forward, she insisted that Connor was ready to move. We packed him up in the car, together with a bin bag full of clothes and toys, and drove him home.

Connor settled quite quickly. The health visitor came out to see him within a couple of days and noted that the toys he had come with were a little young for his age. After her visit, Steve headed off to a toy superstore for the first trip of many to this particular retail establishment. Not wanting to overwhelm Connor, we introduced some of the new toys slowly and without making a big deal out of "presents". All very sensible and very controlled as our urge, like any new parents, would be to give our son presents with great joy.

About a week after Connor moved to us, we had a difficult and emotional situation to deal with. The social workers insisted that his foster carer come and visit him in his home "to show Connor that she had not left him". This was horrific. She was as lovely as ever, bringing over a gorgeous panda soft toy and being delighted to see him.

However, after she left Connor became agitated and upset, and simply shook with a complete lack of understanding of what had just happened. He was, after all, only 21 months old, how could he be expected to understand.

It was now late July 2006 and after 19 months in the process we had our son; thank goodness a natural pregnancy doesn't last that long. Steve managed a couple of weeks off work on paternity leave and I was on adoption leave. We spent those two weeks getting used to the addition to our family. Despite all the preparation, we really had no idea what to do now. Toddler groups were not something mentioned to us during the preparation phase, let alone nursery or school placements. Like all new parents we just found out as we went along.

Our neighbour at the top of our track (we live rather rurally) had a son a month younger than Connor so she kindly suggested I go with her to the local toddler group. Like all new parents, I met other parents and we chatted about experiences. For some time, I remember feeling a bit of a fraud. I had no experience to discuss, this was it, 21 months old and our new son. I remember watching him – at that age the children play alongside each other rather than with each other, but Connor was different, he was just that bit further detached from the play, pottering on his own with a toy, usually a toy car that was fascinating him at that time. I put it down to his early life experience and recent move from the safety of familiar surroundings.

Our second son

In some ways, all parents learn from their experiences of parenting their first child, whether the child is born naturally or whether they are adopted. With some experience of the system of adopting a child we decided that we would like to adopt again. Around March 2007, we approached the adoption service and were told that we would be required to go through a second approval process. Furthermore, we could not start this until our son had been with us for a year, but in our case, that would be the October. I never quite understood this. Connor was placed with us in the July of the previous year so that meant a period of 15 months before a second application and process would commence. We questioned this at the time but received no response as to why it would be 15 months in our case.

We made it clear that we wanted to progress matters and that we wanted a change of social worker appointed to us. During the assessment process we had two social workers, one we liked and trusted and one we did not take to. There was no reason, perhaps other than a bit of a cloak-and-dagger attitude to information; the situation with the "Form E" was a perfect example. The request was granted and, in fact, the other of the two social workers from the original assessment was appointed. We felt more comfortable going forward on this basis. The process started all over again – visits to our house, further questions and reports were all completed, but thankfully in a slightly shorter time period. We were approved to adopt a second child and then the waiting started again. This time the wait was much shorter and an approach was made to us to consider Stephen. This time we had sight of the forms containing the information required to make such a decision.

Stephen's early life is a heartbreaking story. Stephen was taken into care a week short of his first birthday, unable to move his arms and legs after suffering serious neglect. He was malnourished and arrived at his foster carers in an emaciated state, something that to this day Gill, his most wonderful foster carer, remembers with emotion. Stephen was born in the Royal Hospital for Sick Children in Edinburgh. He had a serious gastric condition called gastroschisis, or in other words his intestines were outside his body. He also had only one functioning kidney and a mass in place of his other kidney. With life-saving surgery conducted shortly after birth, Stephen should have been a high priority for the care service to ensure his future well-being.

He was placed with Gill just before his first birthday, she and her family cared for this little chap and did everything in their power to support and nourish his development during the time he stayed with them. For this we are forever grateful.

It was around Easter time 2008 when the social worker called us and said that they had a possible match for us, a little boy who had been in care for almost 11 months, he was approaching his second birthday. We were told a little about his situation and we were encouraged to visit the doctor who had been appointed to do a medical on Stephen for more information. I remember quite vividly sitting in a room in a medical practice with this doctor looking at medical notes and discussing what she knew of Stephen's background and the chances of him having difficulties in the future. It was all rather vague, lots of maybes and not a great deal of fact. Looking back, we could and should have asked more pertinent questions, particularly whether there were any drugs or alcohol involved, genetic conditions or developmental difficulties. But we sat there while the doctor flicked through the notes and possibilities about future care.

We talked and considered the information provided to us and, as you will no doubt guess, we decided to go ahead. The social worker told us not to tell Connor until much closer to the time. Again we thought this was strange and felt that any decision to tell Connor or our family about our future should be our decision.

The legal matters took much longer than we had hoped for and it was not until the August that we finally met our son. His foster carer and I had talked on the phone on numerous occasions and by the time I finally met her we felt we had a strong bond and a determination to make sure the introductions and move to our care went without difficulty. She took the lead regarding a plan for the introductions and she made it very clear that she felt this little boy should be moved quickly to our care. From our point of view and from experience, we were keen to undertake a quick transition, for the sake of both Stephen and Connor.

Despite this approach, the social work service decided that introductions would take a minimum of seven days and that Stephen could not be moved into our care before the full seven-day period had taken place. There were still legal matters to complete, particularly the change of residency. A date was set for this hearing, so we started introductions seven days beforehand with the hope that the hearing would go in favour of the change and Stephen could be moved to our house. Thankfully it did.

The foster carer was so right, Stephen was more than ready to move to us by the fourth day, but we continued to visit and take him out as per the plan. On the day of

over to Gill's house to collect
le boy she had looked after for
d her goodbyes and headed off
at home for her call to tell us
in our favour. Stephen would
ver family.

d her family were wonderful
e of Stephen, his background
ʌnu his potential difficulties helped us immensely in the
first few years and is still relevant to his current care.
We look at Stephen today and see a young boy, now 11
years old, who struggles in an educational environment
but has come on so much given his start in life. He will,
I am sure, need care and guidance throughout his life,
but it is certainly thanks to his wonderful foster family
that we see not only difficulties but also his potential
in life. He has an encyclopaedic knowledge of sharks,
dinosaurs, Marvel characters and various films, he
watches National Geographic documentaries with as
much interest as watching *Spiderman*. I saw a wonderful
post on Facebook recently, next to an image of C-3PO
from *Star Wars*. It said, "According to my calculations,
autistic children that have acquired immense knowledge
of a subject should have that knowledge acknowledged
as expertise, not an obsessive interest."[1]

Completing our family

About a week before we were due to meet Stephen, we
received a call from the social work service suggesting

---

[1] https://www.facebook.com/AutismOdysseys/

that we stop the process for Stephen and wait for Connor's natural sibling, who was now about a month old. We could not believe it. Stephen had been given photographs of us and of Connor, preparing him for his move to his Mummy and Daddy. Connor was also being prepared to have a brother. How could we do such a thing to either child? We declined and insisted on continuing with the introductions and adoption of Stephen. We suggested that when the time came, and the legal process was to a point that Connor's sibling would be moved to a permanent family, they should consider contacting us.

The next few months we concentrated on and put every effort into our two boys, Connor and Stephen. We heard nothing from social services about the baby, how things were progressing or whether, in fact, the baby would be placed for adoption. It was around eight months after Stephen was placed with us that, completely out of the blue, we received a telephone call from social services asking if they could come and see us about Harry, Connor's natural sibling.

The previous few months had been interesting. Shortly after Stephen was placed with us, I managed to rupture a ligament in my wrist, which left the wrist requiring reconstruction. I had been in plaster for around 13 weeks and had managed to learn how to change Stephen's nappy one armed. Having recovered from the injury, the prospect of having a third child seemed quite easy.

Like Connor, Harry had been in care since birth and had been the subject of a Child Protection Order. He had been placed with a foster carer shortly after birth. The whole process should have been simple, we already had Harry's older sibling and things should have been set to progress quite smoothly. How wrong that turned out to be. There were numerous hurdles to jump.

Harry was reported to be a happy and healthy baby. He was living with a family in Inverkeithing, Fife. There were no concerns at all about his health and well-being. We agreed to go ahead and have ourselves put forward to an adoption panel for formal matching. Difficulties then started with the social workers attempting to get parental permission for the adoption to make life simpler. We were told we would be required to meet the maternal grandmother, who had indicated that she would be able to get her daughter to sign the papers. Unfortunately, Steve was away on business and therefore only I could go along to a social work office where a meeting had been arranged. It was so evident from early on that there was no relationship between this woman and her daughter and, in fact, all she was after was a photograph of Connor. It was disturbing and made us even more conscious to ensure our children's safety going forward. Interestingly, however, it would also be fair to say that I felt no connection between our son and this person, it was like talking to a stranger who was unconnected to us in every way.

As it turned out, the adoption panel meeting was also not plain sailing. The members of the panel had not been pleased that the meeting with the maternal grandmother, arranged by the social workers, had taken place prior to their decision. I had attended this panel meeting at the request of the social worker to respond to any questions they might have. After facing extensive questioning about our family and how we would cope with a third child, I was asked to leave while they contemplated their decision. A considerable length of time later, the social worker came out to say that the meeting had gone in our favour for formal matching, but there had been considerable discussion on various points. It turned out not to have been a unanimous decision. One of the Panel members had cared for Stephen for respite care for a week previously. She had the view that we would not be able to cope with an additional child. Clearly not impartial, and had the decision not been in our favour, certainly grounds for appeal.

After all this you would think that things could progress, and they did. Harry was placed with us after the usual introductions. That was interesting. It was clear during the introductions that Harry had been cared for by a relation of the foster carer on a regular basis. It was also evident that Harry had been "promised" to her by the foster carer who also sat on adoption panels. All extremely strange and quite a tricky environment for us to introduce our two other children to their new brother. During the introductions the foster carer made the whole process extremely difficult; the details need to remain private but certainly a different experience again. At the end of the introductory period there was the usual hearing for a change of residency. In Connor's case this meant that he would go home with us from his foster carer's house. In Stephen's case, Steve collected him from his foster carer on the morning of the hearing. In Harry's case he was handed over in a car park in Glenrothes.

About two months after Harry had been placed with us, the legal process for adoption was continuing without concern until we received information that the maternal grandfather had come forward and was making a claim as an alternative carer for Harry. What a stressful time for us. The legal process had to be stopped while social services assessed this person as a potential carer. We were also advised to engage the services of a lawyer to act on our behalf.

During Connor's adoption we came across a lawyer who had been appointed by the court to act in Connor's interests. She had visited our house and quite simply was lovely. Steve and I agreed that we should approach her to act on our behalf, feeling that she already had a brief knowledge of us and of our eldest son. I phoned her office and spoke with her, and she was delighted to hear from us and to learn about Connor's progress. As the conversation went on she realised that she could not act for us, nor comment further, as she had been appointed by the court to represent the other party. She recommended a colleague, also very experienced in family law. Before the phone call finished she did put my mind a little at rest by indicating (but without saying so) that the process would be a formality and not to worry.

There was hearing after hearing and as time progressed the legal process to adopt a child under Scottish law changed, just to complicate matters further. All this time Harry was in our care. We had been told that he was fit and well and there were no medical concerns. However, shortly after he was placed with us it became evident that he had an inguinal hernia, which had first been noticed when he was a few months old but not dealt with (we found an entry in his "red book" of health visits to this effect). The hernia kept coming through his abdominal wall and having been referred to the Royal Hospital for Sick Children in Edinburgh, we were told he would require surgery. Our GP had shown me how to push the hernia back when it came through, and I was having to do this on a daily basis.

When Harry was around 16 months old, the hernia came through and despite all efforts I could not push it back. He was a poorly little boy. Steve was in Japan at the time and I left our two other boys with my mum and drove Harry to Edinburgh. I remember arriving in the Accident and Emergency area and being taken straight through to a cubicle. A young doctor came along and decided to give Harry some morphine. Not willing to wait for the nurse to assist, he had five attempts to get an IV line into Harry's hand and then arm. Quite distressing for all concerned. The sister arrived to find out what had happened and the young doctor was duly dismissed to let the sister take over. After the morphine was administered the hernia was pushed back and Harry looked a great deal more comfortable. He had surgery the next morning as an emergency admission. I remember phoning the social worker as he was still, at this stage, a "looked-after child". She said that she would check for permissions for the surgery, though by this time he had already been taken to theatre.

After much toing and froing, the day of the court hearing arrived. This was a new experience, to say the least. Connor's adoption had been granted in the Sheriffs' chambers, in our absence, and we only found out a couple of days later. Stephen's adoption, again granted in chambers, had been in our presence and with Stephen there. That had been quite a quick experience as Stephen had been rather intrigued by the china tea cups on a tray in the corner of the chambers, and after at least two tea cups had been knocked over, the Sheriff signed the paperwork and wished us the very best of luck. Harry's adoption would see us in a court hearing waiting for the other party to appear and be represented.

Steve was away on business. I met our social worker beforehand and headed into the Sheriff's court offices to meet up with the lawyer acting for us. I remember at the time he said to follow his lead, not to speak unless spoken to directly by the Sheriff, and whatever he (the lawyer) said, not to react at all.

We were the first case to be heard under the new law and, to be perfectly honest, none of us expected the adoption to be granted that day. The paperwork had been submitted and as we waited in the courtroom (the social worker had not been allowed in), I remember feeling quite sick at the thought of what would happen next. The Sheriff entered, we stood. The other party had not arrived. The Sheriff sat and read through the paperwork slowly, saying nothing. He then asked the lawyer a few questions, contemplated quietly again, a few more questions, and then he granted the adoption order. He wished me all the very best and then he left the courtroom. That was it, over in a few rather long minutes. All the months of hearings, reviews, paperwork on hold, and now we had our third son, legally and fully ours.

The legal process

Adopting in Scotland means that we adopted under Scottish law. The legal process is certainly a complicated one and for us the process changed mid-way through adopting our third son.

As you would imagine, the circumstances in which a child finds themselves in care can differ considerably. It is rare nowadays that a child is voluntarily given up for adoption and as such children that are in the care system often come from a very difficult start in life. Our own children are an example, both Connor and Harry taken at birth and subject to Child Protection Orders for their own safety, Stephen neglected and in such an emaciated state that he could not properly move his arms and legs. What does that mean for the legal process? Cases can be complicated and challenged before a permanence order can be granted. Effectively the local authority applies to the court for a permanence order that removes the parental rights from the natural parents and places them with the local authority. Crucially, this then allows the local authority to apply for the child to be adopted and the adoption can be granted without parental consent. This is what happened in Harry's case as he was legally adopted after the Adoption and Children (Scotland) Act 2007 changes came into force.

Both Connor and Stephen followed a different process. Connor was freed for adoption, which was like a permanence order. Stephen was different, he was not freed, but the adoption was a direct petition, with permission given. As you will see from reading this short section, the legal process is a complicated one and it will differ depending on where you adopt. My advice to anyone wishing to embark on this process is to find out as much as you can about the legal process in the country in which you are adopting. In addition, the adoption agency's processes, what you will have to go through, what hearings you will attend and which ones you will not attend. Be prepared to be confused and feel like you are on a legal rollercoaster. It will come together in the end, but not without considerable emotion and stress along the way.

Chapter 2

IS MY CHILD DIFFERENT?

It's because he's adopted

AS THIS CHAPTER progresses, the theme that I hope to show you is how our children's behaviours became different from those of others. When I speak about this now as "not being normal", Connor will shout me down and say there is no such thing as normal. He is quite right. Now at secondary school, his teacher, who specialises in teaching children like Connor, with an autistic spectrum diagnosis or other similar difficulties, has made it very clear to the children in his class that "normal" is not an acceptable term. They are simply not neuro-typical. Which means they think and act in a different way for a great deal of the time. The skill for us as parents is to understand how they are thinking, what is firing their neurons and quite frankly what is not. Recently, I had taken the boys to a trampoline park and one of Connor's classmates was there and came over. He tapped Connor on the shoulder and then stood next to him. The boys smiled at each other, but conversation was like pulling teeth – both boys clearly autistic and wanting to join in but simply struggling with social interaction. In the end, they managed a few words and agreed to go into the trampoline park together. It was quite a moment to reflect on the differences between a neuro-typical child and one who is on the spectrum.

For much of the first few years of each of the boys' lives, I had thought how lucky we had been to adopt these three wonderful boys with no difficulties. In the early years, any differences that were obvious or questionable behaviours I simply put down to the fact that they were adopted. I cannot remember the number of times I used adoption as an excuse for something that they did and that I did not understand.

Each of the boys certainly had a "difficult" start to their life. For Connor and Harry, being in care from birth meant that the most difficult change would be to move to their adoptive family. For Harry, being only 11 months old, the transition from foster care to permanence was certainly easier than it was for Connor. At 21 months, the baby has become a toddler and the attachment to the single foster carer was that much more evident. For Stephen, it was certainly a difficult start: life-saving surgery, neglect, being taken into care and placed with foster carers, 15 months in care and then to his permanent home, it must have had an effect. I think the proper title would be an "attachment disorder", although we have never felt the need to pursue any formal diagnosis. It would be extremely complicated to identify the behaviours in isolation from his other difficulties and we do not feel that there is any burning need to do so. When I think back to the preparation group before we were approved to adopt, I remember the discussion on attachment disorder. It left me rather frightened as to whether I would have a proper parental relationship with my child. Stephen is the most loving of children and very attached to us as his parents. He has a fear of being left and needs reassurance to go anywhere or do anything different from his normal routine. When he does, he usually says something about considering himself very brave. I need not have been at all worried about the love we give to our children and the reciprocal love they give us.

As you read through this chapter, you will see there are times when the situations described could apply to any child, adopted or in the care of a natural parent or parents. Yet there are others where the behaviours start to hint towards something a little more problematic. The benefit of hindsight would have been wonderful in the early years. It might have meant that difficulties could have been identified earlier, particularly for Connor, which might just have meant that we and others might have handled situations with a greater level of knowledge and understanding.

In just under three years from Connor's placement with us, we had three beautiful boys, all under the age of five. Now for any parent that is a handful. It all happened so quickly on reflection, we were a two (just Steve and I), then a three, a four and a five. Our family grew so quickly I am not sure we were really prepared for what was to follow. Mornings and evenings were, and still are, a military operation. When the boys were younger, having settled them all in bed, Steve would hand me a glass of wine on the way down the stairs and we would sit and have a quiet meal together and reflect on the day. Bedtime was probably our best parenting at that stage. I think it was because the days were so tiring that we needed the children to be in bed at a certain time to give us some time on our own.

My life was totally consumed by the children and I found it extremely difficult to focus on anything else. I remember the social workers saying during the preparation process and while the children were still "looked after", before all the formal adoptions were complete, that we would need to make time for ourselves. That is easier said than done. Finding a babysitter for three young children is not an easy task, thank goodness for my mum. She used to come over for dinner and then stay for a little, watching television or reading a book while we went out to our cottage (well, it's a conversion to the side of and above our garage) where we have a pool table. It was lovely to play a couple of frames of pool to get away from the responsibilities of parenting for just half an hour or so.

Early play and toddler groups

Shortly after Connor was placed with us for adoption, the health visitor suggested I take Connor to a local toddler group. She gave me the details of a few groups in the area and thought it would be a good way for Connor to meet and be around other children and for me to meet other parents. All very sensible, and those of you who have had young families have probably done the same thing. We went to that group only a couple of times.

I remember walking in with Connor. I am not sure who was more nervous, him or me. All these mums with their pushchairs and the bags of spare clothes, nappies, wet wipes and stickiness. I did not know what to say to anyone. The questions came thick and fast: How old is your son? Have you moved into the area? I just had to say that we were adopting Connor and this was his first time at a playgroup. He was a little over 22 months old and like all toddlers around that age did not really interact with others. But he was different. The group was held in the village hall and Connor headed for the stage, where there were cupboards underneath, and he kept going in them and then out again. I am not sure what I thought at the time except perhaps that he had never been in such a situation before and simply did not know what to do. The group's organiser kept asking me to take him out of the cupboard, but I did not really know how to do that, he just kept going back. The next week he did the same thing, headed straight for the stage area and the cupboard. He showed no interest in the other children, only the toy cars that he would climb in to and push round. On reflection, I think I would have quite liked to have joined him in the cupboard, the whole experience was rather intimidating, I felt totally out of place. I muddled on through and could not wait until the session was over and we could head home in the car. Was this what parenting was about?

It was shortly after this that our neighbour got in touch and suggested we go with her and her son to another group. It was a lot friendlier. I guess in all walks of life there are places that make you feel welcome and ones that simply do not. This baby and toddler group was indeed a great deal more welcoming than my first foray into the parenting arena.

As I hinted in Chapter 1, attending these groups, particularly at the early stages of having Connor, left me feeling a bit of a fraud. Everyone had stories of their parenting experience, of childbirth, of siblings, nurseries and the like. Connor had been with us for just a few weeks, he was not a babe in arms, and I didn't have any of those stories to tell. I did enjoy meeting some of the people and became quite active in the group and its organisation over the next couple of years. But what about Connor? He went along to this group and seemed to enjoy himself. He played with the same toys each week, usually the cars and trains, and I saw him develop alongside others of a similar age. I say alongside, and that is perhaps what stood out the most. He did not really learn to play with children in the same way that others were doing.

I remember my neighbour bringing her son to play in the garden one afternoon. All I could think was how different these two boys were and how much the adoption process must have affected Connor. They were playing, not together but more alongside each other. The other child was amazing, he communicated so well with his mum and with me, he had great physical movement and he did not seem to be so repetitive in his behaviour. My neighbour had brought down their old toddler slide for Connor to have. Connor was very excited and just went up and down the slide for ages. He was not aware of the other child, just that there was someone there. I kept thinking that he must not have experienced this type of social interaction in foster care; basically I thought, "It's because he's adopted."

After the legalities of the adoption were completed we had a most joyous occasion, Connor's baptism. He was certainly not a baby being held in the arms of a parent at the baptism font, in fact he was exactly two-and-a-half years old on the day of his baptism. It was in April and the weather was unusually warm for the time of year. Steve had turned 40 the day before so it was a super weekend, a real celebration of family life, and our very best friends came up from the south of England to join us. On the Sunday morning, during the weekly morning service, Rt Rev Dr Robert Gillies (or Bob to everyone who knows him) welcomed Connor to the church and baptised him. He handled it all rather well, Connor that is, especially considering what we know now. The service was followed by a party at our house when neighbours and friends came and celebrated our family. I remember the wonderful scene of tables and chairs in the garden and Connor riding his electric quad bike around each of the tables, forming a little circuit. He still had very few words at this point and I cannot remember him speaking to anyone, just riding around until the battery finally died.

Connor's third birthday, his second in our care, was a memorable occasion. I had invited his "friends" from the toddler group. Which basically meant I had invited a group of adults whom I had met over the last year or so with children of a similar age. The party was at our house and consisted of around 14 children on a massive "play date". I had produced the standard party food for the kids and even made a cake in the shape of a combine harvester, something that I am still rather proud of if truth be known. Connor was quite obsessed with farm machinery at this stage of his life, not unlike many of the children that live around here. Not only did I cater for the children, but I thought it would be nice to cater for the adults as well. So, a homemade curry and rice was prepared the day before and ready for when the kids had consumed their party food. Connor sat at the table in a prominent position, ate the party food with the other children and then didn't leave the table when the adults' turn arrived. He managed a large plate of curry and naan bread.

What about Stephen and Harry? Stephen arrived with us at the age of two years three months and was clearly developmentally delayed. He came with Connor and I to "toddlers" and again played alongside other children, mostly just with the Brio train set and the ride-in cars. By this point, I thought that everything was quite normal; yes, he was developmentally delayed, but this was all due to his start in life and he would "catch up". Stephen didn't really develop that fast in the early stages after placement with us. He was a very emotional child and had physical issues, including difficulties with proprioception, which basically meant that he had difficulty knowing where his arms and legs were in space. He fell over constantly, almost from a standing position at times, knocked things over, such as cups of juice, and generally appeared rather clumsy. Any visit to the local supermarket normally ended with something being knocked over, even when he was riding in the trolley. Strangely enough, as I write this, only this week did we take the boys out for fish and chips at a local restaurant and Stephen had a glass of Coke which ended up all over the floor. Stephen still is a very emotional child. He has difficulties with emotional regulation in that it appears to be all or nothing. Something that upsets him will cause catastrophic tears and crying. Generally, however, the problem, whatever it is, can be resolved quickly and he becomes happy again.

Harry arrived with us around nine months after us having Stephen. What a happy child he was, rarely crying and basically smiling his way around the world. He was the easy one. He came along to the toddler group for a while, but by this time, with three children under five years old, I had begun to think that perhaps I needed some time to myself. I also noticed that some of the adults around me were acting differently. I had managed to get in with a small group of mums of the other toddlers, but Harry's arrival had caused some issues for them. Apparently – and I only found this out later – some had been a little envious of our growing family and had thought that it was just too easy for us.

Anyway, this group of mums took turns to host coffee mornings, where the adults had coffee and cake and the children had an opportunity to play, with some snacks provided. Very civilised. It was strange watching my children play around the other children. They were different. I remember one occasion where a couple of the boys a year and two years older than Connor came down to complain that Connor was annoying them. I jumped up and tried to get Connor to come away and play with something else, without thinking that anything else could be wrong. Stephen was also different in this group of children, so developmentally delayed that he really couldn't play with them at all. He simply pottered alongside and kept a very close eye on me for much of the time.

Connor had started school, Stephen had started nursery and Harry was at home with me. Harry was far more adaptable than the other boys, so I started playing a bit of golf again. Well, what that really meant was I took my golf clubs to the driving range, parked Harry's buggy behind me and hit a basket of balls while Harry drank his milk and had a snooze. Quite idyllic really.

Attending nursery

The term after his third birthday, Connor started nursery at the local school. The very experienced nursery teacher welcomed all the new little ones and another chapter in Connor's life opened. In fact, I remember her meeting Connor beforehand in the butcher's shop in the village of Crail. She spoke to him and he looked straight past her, concentrating on the meat display on the counter.

I think he enjoyed nursery. By this stage Connor had become interested in words and their meaning, so each morning we tried to find a new word for him to learn and include in his vocabulary. I thought this was quite nice, but the nursery teacher seemed to not really take on board his interest in language. I remember her saying, "We think it is more important to get Connor to look at us when talking." Of course, Connor did give me eye contact, but rarely did he look at others when speaking. I just thought it was shyness or a lack of confidence. With what we know now, this would be an indicator that things might not be neuro-typical.

Connor continued to play around people, with very little imaginative play. He liked to play with cars and trains, basically pushing them around. By this time, I had started to see differences between him and other children. I put it down to his start in life, the lack of social interaction at a young age, quite frankly "it's because he's adopted". I cannot say how many times I must have justified situations with that phrase, but what else could it be?

The nursery provided both a short break for me and for Connor an opportunity to explore the world, albeit rather differently than others. He was particularly interested in the small outdoor pond that had been created in the nursery garden.

I remember that one day we had seen lobster pots outside a house. Fascinated by these, we had gone home and looked up all about how to catch a lobster. The next day at nursery one of the early years officers, who was acting in place of the nursery teacher, grabbed the opportunity and with the children set up a display including a lobster pot that they had at the school. She reported that this was wonderful for Connor – he engaged and spoke to other children in a manner that he had not done before. I am not sure who was more excited, her, Connor or me.

Connor left nursery and started school right before his fifth birthday. Stephen then embarked on his life at nursery, the same nursery as Connor initially. Stephen was not dry at this stage and needed to stay in nappies or pull-ups. The pressure on mums and children to ensure they are dry starting nursery is so great, particularly with children who have had a difficult or unsettled start in life. The nursery agreed to take Stephen and to change him if necessary. A very likeable little boy, Stephen was still quite clearly delayed in his development, but he managed to cope with going to nursery, despite his anxieties when I left him each morning.

I had met up with another mum at toddlers. Like me she had three young children and wanted a little more time for herself. Her middle daughter was the same age as Harry and they had formed a lovely friendship. We found the most wonderful private nursery and decided that both children would go together a couple of mornings each week. It was super, they enjoyed themselves immensely, Harry still talks about his time there and all the people he met and the adults who looked after him. He is now nine years old and that in itself is a compliment to the nursery staff.

For Stephen, the nursery teacher was retiring at the end of Stephen's first year in nursery and there had been many parties and occasions to celebrate her career. This effectively meant that the early years officers were running the nursery and were short-staffed. On two occasions, I had picked Stephen up from nursery and he had been wet and then dried in the warm sunshine while playing outside. Not surprisingly, Stephen left that nursery shortly afterwards and joined Harry at the private nursery.

Stephen and Harry both enjoyed themselves immensely at this nursery, with activities inside and outdoors, collecting eggs from chickens and walks around the rural location. The staff were excellent and thoroughly understood both boys. At this stage Harry was not showing any signs of difficulty. Stephen, however, was clearly developmentally delayed and presented some challenges to the staff. When I arrived to collect the boys one day I recall one of the nursery staff asking to have a word with me. Apparently, she had taken her eyes off Stephen for just a moment and he had managed to strip off all his clothes and was standing in the water tray, splashing away as though it was a paddling pool. This became a theme for a while, even on a wintery day with the snow coming down heavily outside, all the children wrapped up warm and throwing snowballs, then Stephen appeared from the playhouse with no clothes and announcing it was rather cold.

With its location just outside St Andrews, Steve often dropped the boys on his way to work. With three young children, this worked well as it left me to take Connor to school. It is certainly true that once you have more than two children as a couple you are outnumbered. With three children so young I simply didn't have enough hands to cope. Nowadays, I love the reruns of the sit-com "Outnumbered" – I can so relate to some of the ridiculous conversations that occur in the household, especially the middle child's differences with the world around him.

Starting school

I remember going to a parents' open evening at the local school prior to Connor starting the next term. The head teacher and the class teacher were present, the head teacher doing a short introduction welcoming all the new parents and saying hello to some familiar faces, those who already had older children at the school. She then handed over to the class teacher, who attempted to explain what the day would look like for the new primary one children and what type of schoolwork they would do. I came away from that evening with a sinking feeling. Rather than being excited for my son, I left with the feeling that there would be little structure. She was a teacher of many years' standing, teaching at the young end of school for a considerable time. Yet when asked questions about the children learning to read, for example, she held up some of the books in the reading range and kept saying they were "lovely books". The word "lovely" appeared in nearly every sentence and it all seemed a little wishy-washy, for want of a better phrase.

I wish I could find the report that the nursery teacher wrote on Connor to share with you. However, from memory, it was a full summary of what Connor was like, what his needs were moving from nursery into school life, his interests and basically what made him tick. I remember reading it thinking that the nursery teacher could not have done a better job. Connor was, and still is, a child who enjoys facts and information based on real things. He has a thirst for knowledge and school should have been the starting blocks for him to blossom.

I came away from Connor's first parents' evening in tears. Connor was struggling to settle into a classroom environment. He was unable to sit on the carpet in the morning, listen to instructions, complete tasks and behave in an "appropriate" manner. I could not work out what was wrong. After just a few weeks at school I was called in by the deputy head teacher to talk about Connor's behaviour. Connor was present in the room and he sat in the chair, swinging his legs backwards and forwards with a defiant look on his face. It was awful. I had never seen him looking like that. If I only knew then what I know now, I am sure that I would have handled matters very differently. I remember travelling home, being angry and raising my voice to him. This did not improve things at all. From then on, the teacher called me in or spoke to me at the door nearly every afternoon to report on Connor's behaviour. There was even a letter from the deputy head teacher to tell me that Connor had pulled an older girl's hair in the playground. Interestingly, and looking back now, that was the start of blaming him for situations without getting to the root cause; the girl in question had in fact taken the ball Connor and his friend were playing with.

One afternoon I was called in and the teacher explained that there had been a problem in school. Connor was fine, but he might have a sore arm that evening. I was horrified: what had happened? Connor had been made to sit on the carpet with the class but had been sitting next to the radiator. He put his arm behind the radiator for whatever reason and it had become stuck. The poor little boy had his arm stuck for an hour, buckets of soapy water and the janitor trying to remove the radiator from the wall, without luck. His arm eventually dislodged just as they were picking up the phone for the fire service to come and help. If only the school had called me. Connor must have been traumatised by the situation; he was certainly a very quiet little thing that evening.

Connor's behaviour at school continued to be problematic. Picking up Stephen from nursery at lunchtime, I would see Connor sitting on the wall in the playground next to the supervisor for yet another "time out". It was heartbreaking.

About a week before the end of the school year we had noticed that Connor was even less of himself. I had taken him to the local swimming pool in St Andrews and we had a wonderful time. Walking out to the car, with his brothers and my mum, who had been giving me a hand with them, a slightly older boy shouted out, "Hello Connor" across the car park. Connor went quiet, walked to the other side of the car and got in. I asked him why he hadn't answered, and he refused to speak. Rather strange. We headed off to a local fruit farm to meet up with friends. Connor got out of the car and headed down to see the farm animals. He didn't speak to anyone for at least an hour.

That weekend, out to the supermarket with Steve, Connor started to open up about his experiences at school and the fact that the boy across the car park had been pushing him around. In fact, it was later that evening when he was having a bath that we noticed bruises on the inside of his ankles and on parts of his legs that were not from a child being boisterous in his play, he had been kicked. Steve and I added two and two together and we certainly came up with the right answer. How could we have missed all the signs, physical as well as emotional indicators? I think it had been going on for some time; in fact, one of the other young children said so in the end. I feel so strongly that the adults around Connor let him down in that first year of school life.

Into school on the Monday morning I headed straight for the head teacher's office. After a rather extensive discussion it was clear that the school would not accept the fact that Connor was being bullied. I was distraught and we decided over the summer holidays that a move of school was the only sensible option.

A move to an even smaller rural school just outside St Andrews saw Connor starting his second year in education. On the first day, another child stabbed him in the hand with a pencil. The school was very apologetic, but it set the scene for another year of being called in pretty much every day. More of that later.

Stephen started school the following year. But Stephen was developmentally delayed and as such, visits had been made to the nursery to assess him and decide what level of support he would require. A pupil support assistant was appointed to be with him at school. Everyone loved him, the cute little boy with blond hair and an engaging smile. Life at school was easy for Stephen. Although he continued to suffer from anxiety when I left him, as many children do with their parents taking them to school, Stephen loved being with the other children. He was the only primary one student in the school and was doted on by both staff and children alike.

I am not sure whether he learned very m...
first year but he had a lovely time. He was, an...
very small for his age. At this stage he continued t...
problems with just knowing where his hands and feet v...
(proprioception). One call home was memorable. Th...
poor little thing had been blown over in the wind and had
hit his nose and put his teeth through his lip. By the time I
arrived at the school, he was cuddled into the pupil support
assistant, whose coat was soaked in Stephen's blood.

Harry's start into school life was uneventful. His
entire nursery education was at the private nursery,
which did everything possible to prepare the children for
school. Home-cooked meals, visits to the farm, lots of
outdoor play, what more could a young boy want? After
a couple of visits to the school during the previous term,
Harry started in primary one with the kindest and most
lovely teacher. He blossomed in his first year of primary
education and we continued to think that he was the
"normal" one of the family.

Why is he behaving this way?

Just after Stephen was placed for adoption with us, I
had a couple of weeks away from home. I had been
asked, for the second time, to captain an England golf
team at the World Amateur Team Championships in
Australia. I had been due to attend the Championships
in South Africa in the same capacity two years earlier,
but we had been advised that we would be having
Connor and I had to withdraw at late notice. When
the letter came through again, Steve and I talked about
it and decided that he would manage on his own for a
couple of weeks with both boys.

struggled. It was not so much
...as the problem; Connor started
..." behaviour and Steve found
...rrived home with presents, as
...'t-toy kangaroos. Stephen had
...le of months and then I had
...ould be tough given his start
...nor we thought was more settled and we
...re surprised by his behaviour during and afterwards. It
had to be because he's adopted, we told ourselves.

I remember bath times with Connor and Stephen,
everything had to follow the same pattern each time.
Another military operation to add to the day. I will
never forgive Stephen's foster carer for sending him to us
with onesies that had poppers all the way up the front. It
took me for ever to get a wriggling and giggling Stephen
into that thing. Off to the shop for normal pyjamas was
a certainty.

It was shortly after that trip to Australia that I
was in the bathroom with Connor. He had just had
a shower and was being extremely difficult about
getting his pyjamas on. I went to pick him up and he
twisted and my wrist "popped". I say popped because
that's what it sounded like. I finished up and went
downstairs, said to Steve, "I think I have really hurt
my wrist." Now toddlers have tantrums and the injury
to my wrist could have happened at any time and
anywhere. It was probably caused originally by hitting
thousands of golf balls in my younger days. Without
going into the unnecessary details of how and when
it was diagnosed, it turned out that I had managed to
snap the scapholunate ligament and required surgery
to reconstruct the wrist.

So now we had two young boys and me unable to drive and living in a rural location where a car is a necessity. It was a tricky few weeks and months while the wrist repaired. Nevertheless, we managed. Fortunately, Connor was still in nursery at that stage, so a neighbour kindly stepped in and took him to and from nursery each morning. Other than that, I was one-armed and housebound with two very young children to look after, one still in nappies.

Having recovered from my wrist injury I now had one child at school, one at a state nursery attached to the school and one at home. Life was moving on. We had been told a little of Stephen's start in life, not the full picture by any means, but we understood more of his behaviour than Connor's.

But why, and what was so difficult about Connor's behaviour at that time? I remember being confused then and I still am. Connor started his second year at school at a different and smaller rural school. He didn't play in the playground with the other children, he dug in the dirt at the side of the playing field for much of his break and lunchtimes. I thought this behaviour was particularly odd. I couldn't understand why he didn't seem to make friends with the other children, or play with them in a way that you would generally see children playing in a school playground; perhaps running around playing "tag" or playing football with the other boys. No, Connor would be digging with his hands in the dirt.

The teacher was an older lady with many years' experience. There had been no mention of any possible links to autistic spectrum behaviour. When Connor was not acting appropriately, he was just naughty. The teacher isolated him in the classroom and I later discovered that much of the time she acted in a manner that would probably be considered as bullying. I was called into school pretty much every day. Stephen and Harry were both still at nursery at this stage and my mum would come over to the house in the afternoons to sit with them while I picked Connor up from school, aware that it usually took some time as I was invariably called into discuss the behaviour of the day. He wouldn't line up with the other children, he failed to follow instructions, he would head to the toilets and wet paper towels. One pupil support assistant had witnessed him squashing up the paper towels in his hands. She suggested that Connor, in behaving in this way, was attempting to gain as much sensory information as possible. The teacher dismissed this, saying Connor was just naughty. I had very little to offer the teacher at these meetings, I simply could not understand what we were doing wrong as parents – we were trying our hardest to teach our son how to behave, to understand what was expected of him. It was not working. The behaviour was odd. As I was writing this all down, I thought I would ask Connor whether he remembered wetting the paper towels. He smiled and said he did, he didn't really know why except that it felt nice. He also said that when he panicked about doing it he would put them down the toilet and then the toilet would overflow. Even the feeling of the water on the floor with the paper towels was comforting in some way.

As you now know, Stephen was and is developmentally delayed. His behaviours were also not typical of a similar-aged child but were far easier to understand and to forgive. Having knowledge of a child's potential difficulties even at an early stage gives you some understanding of what is going on. Stephen started school with the adults around him knowing that he would have difficulties.

Stephen had one rather unusual display of behaviour that rather amused the adults around him, although he was still "in trouble" with the head teacher. The class had been working on a special project (I can't remember what the subject was), but in the corner of the classroom was a display using quite a lot of tissue paper. Stephen had gone to the display and one of the pieces of tissue had torn; we think hearing the sound was attractive to him. He proceeded to karate chop the entire area, hearing the tissue paper tear around him; he was in his own very special world.

Understanding the differences

I look back on those nursery and early school years with more understanding of what was going on than I ever had at the time. I suppose that is always the same in life, we look back and say what we would have done if we knew then what we know now. When we embarked on the adoption process, we just wanted a family. We always knew that our children would be different, they were adopted after all, but we had no idea about how different they would be. We were ill-informed as to their genetic background and any early displays of behaviour that would have suggested a difficulty were not investigated. I think back to meeting Connor, being in the back garden of his foster carer's house and having to spin the garden umbrella repeatedly.

With Stephen, I think Steve and I both knew he would be "different", but his foster carer was so convinced that he would catch up we didn't really worry too much. He is certainly different from other children of his age, not just because he is adopted or because of his start in life. His difficulties and disabilities make his future unknown. We talk about this quite a lot. What will happen in a few years when he becomes an adult?

Harry's pre-school years and first couple of years at school went smoothly. He did not start to display any characteristics of the difficulties he is now diagnosed with until the age of around six. Even now they can be hidden and it is still hard for us to understand them. He was given various diagnoses, but he can also be so "normal" at times. It is those times when we forget that his difficulties seem to show at their worst, almost when our guard is down. Just going out to the local fish and chip restaurant a few weeks ago, somewhere he has been on many occasions. The table we were given was in the heart of the restaurant, in the busiest area. He struggled with the sounds and smells around him, people watching him, looking. It was my idea to go, the boys had all seemed as though they were in a good place and I had thought it would be a nice treat. A perfect example of when we needed all our energies and strategies to contain a situation, two boys loving their fish and chips and one simply not wanting to be there at all. We left the restaurant exhausted. For us, having an understanding that this was not naughty behaviour but behaviour that is directly related to Harry's autism gives us some solace. At these times it is autism that we are dealing with, not the child himself, if that makes any sense at all.

For any parent, understanding your child is so important in providing them with a stable and nurturing upbringing. For us, we need to understand not only the child but the conditions which affect the way in which they can behave. This is not to say that they are not naughty, they certainly can be naughty at times. The skill is deciding when this is.

Chapter 3

WHAT IS WRONG WITH MY CHILD?

Is my child autistic?

For many of you the behavioural situations that I have described are glaringly obvious as characteristics of autism, certainly for our eldest son. However, as a parent with no knowledge whatsoever of the condition, its characteristics and the challenges autistic people and those who care for them face on a day-to-day basis, it was all rather overwhelming when autism was suggested to us. In this chapter I offer an insight into our personal journey through the diagnostic process, not only for autism but for the other conditions that our children suffer from and that we deal with daily.

It was just before Christmas in Connor's third year at school that three people in the space of a week approached me and said something along the lines of "I hope you don't mind, but does Connor have autism?" The first was his swimming teacher, a lovely lady called Kirsty, who had an amazing way with all the children she taught to swim. Connor had been in her swimming class since his first year of school and she seemed to understand him extremely well. The second was a friend, who has three autistic children herself, whom I got to know during the school run in the mornings and afternoons. The third was Connor's teacher, a probationer who had recently been on a course looking at autism in the classroom. She later revealed that during the course all she kept thinking of was Connor and how his behaviours so clearly matched the information she was receiving. She wanted to keep putting her hand up and say, "He's in my class." My reaction to all three was, as you may expect, something along the lines of "Oh no, Connor is adopted, and he has had a tricky start in life." But by the third time it did get me thinking. With no knowledge of the condition at all, I referred to Google, as anyone probably would, and searched the internet for information.

As I sat at my computer in the study at home, looking at the NHS website[2] on autism, I looked down the list of symptoms and signs in school-age children. Connor ticked each box to a greater or lesser extent. I sat looking at the different sections of information and characteristics listed under the titles "spoken language", "responding to others", "interacting with others" and "behaviour". It described my child. I must have read that web page several times with absolutely no idea where to turn next.

Steve arrived home from work that evening and I mentioned to him the three people who had suggested that Connor might be autistic. His reaction was the same as mine, it was because he's adopted. We talked a

---

[2] NHS (National Health Service) (2016) Autism spectrum disorder. Available at www.nhs.uk/conditions/autism/, accessed 30 January 2018.

little about the information I had gained from my rather limited research, but it was a difficult conversation and one that we both needed to think about a little further. I left the web page on the computer and a couple of days later Steve read what I had read that day. It was in the evening and I was cooking us something to eat, having put all the boys to bed. Steve came into the kitchen, announced that he had just read the NHS information and that he was going to the shop for wine because we were going to need it.

At this stage we had absolutely no idea how to progress matters to find out whether Connor was autistic and what that would mean for us and our family. Thinking back, before this point we had sought advice on Connor's behaviour and had been referred to Child and Adolescent Mental Health Services (CAMHS). On several occasions we had attended appointments to discuss Connor but without Connor present; for some reason they did not want to see him. I am still confused by this. In some ways the meetings were quite comforting for us – we spoke openly about Connor and our difficulties in understanding him and his behaviour. But although we felt better having discussed some of the situations we were facing, there did not appear to be a solution on the horizon. After a few meetings it was agreed that one of the child psychotherapists would visit the school to observe Connor's behaviour. After which we heard nothing. A few months later we received a letter stating that as we had not been in touch, the file would be closed.

By this point we were really struggling. Eventually, we received feedback from the observation visits. It was now November 2011 and the visits to the school were in the May. The letter included, "Connor finds it hard to find a way into social games with other children. His desire to engage with others was evident but at times he seemed to struggle to find a helpful way to go about this." The suggested solution was that he join a group such as Beavers or other extracurricular activities which involved lots of interaction with other children. I could not think of anything worse for our son, to force him into a situation that he clearly would be unable to cope with.

So, there we were, CAMHS input had not suggested autism but the observations of others around him and the information on the NHS website certainly suggested that it was an avenue to be investigated. We asked for a referral to the community paediatrician.

It was this first visit to the paediatrician that in some ways set my mind at rest. She had a great deal of experience with autism and was considered an expert in the field. During the visit she observed Connor and explained to me the process for diagnosis, the Autism Spectrum Community Assessment, commonly referred to as the "ASCA pathway". At the end I asked her what she thought and she confirmed that just during this visit she could see autistic traits in Connor that warranted further investigation. The ball started rolling, with forms for us as the parents to fill in, and forms to be filled in and reports written by the school and the class teacher. Visits from speech and language therapists, educational psychology, clinical psychology and community paediatrics. As you would imagine, this all took quite some time. Eventually all the reports were received and a date was set for the final diagnostic meeting.

Filling in the questionnaire on Connor's behaviour was difficult, not only because you read the question and can almost tell by the answer you are giving that it is going to score high on the system, but because of the questions about early development. Connor was 21 months when he came to us – we simply did not know the answers to when he first sat up, when he walked, etc. We were just trying to be a proper family and the fact that we had the children only after they already had some life experience brought back the whole feeling of not quite fulfilling the parental role.

I remember the day well. It was a Wednesday in May 2012. More than six months since the condition was first suggested to us. The meeting would be held at Connor's school, with the head teacher chairing the discussion. The reports of all professionals that had been part of the assessment would be reviewed and considered to determine whether the criteria for an autistic spectrum diagnosis had been reached. As parents we would not be part of the discussion process but would be asked to come in at the end to hear the decision.

At the time of the meeting I was coaching my regular group of lady golfers. Steve went to the school and waited outside the meeting room while the discussion took place. I was on the second tee of the nine-hole course at Elie with the group of golfers when the call came in. Connor met the criteria and now had an autism diagnosis. Steve was a little shaky on the phone, as was I receiving the call. I remember quite vividly standing there on the golf course being told that my son was autistic. The ladies I was with all knew Connor and knew of some of the difficulties we had encountered since adoption. I think they all were a little stunned by the gravitas of the call, and they all still remember that moment well. It was, of course, not a surprise, but autism is a life-long condition for which there is no cure. What impact would this have on us and on the rest of Connor's life?

We decided that we should tell Connor that he had autism and try to explain to him what that meant. I am not sure we really understood it well enough ourselves at this stage. At the diagnostic meeting Steve had been given a pack of information on autism and where to find help and support; leaflets from various societies and charities with information on the condition were included. That was it. Your child has an autism spectrum disorder and here is your pack of information. I am not sure what I expected. Perhaps some form of solution to the problem. Certainly, I was expecting some support for Connor himself at school. But this was not the case. It was just a diagnosis, nothing really changed.

I went online and bought a book aimed at children Connor's age – he was now seven-and-a-half years old. It was titled *I have Autism... What's that?*.[3] I talked to Connor about the diagnosis, explaining that the people who had been to see him had been looking at whether he was autistic. We read the book together and Connor recognised many of the characteristics described. The book stayed in his room for quite a few years and I noticed that at times of stress it had been brought out and re-read.

Nowadays, Connor spends considerable time on the internet searching for people like him; YouTube videos of autism and Asperger's syndrome that describe

---

[3] Doherty K, McNally P, Sherrard E (2001) I Have Autism... What's That?.

characteristics of people he feels he can associate with. Recently the BBC programme about Chris Packham, who has presented wildlife programmes for more than 30 years, titled "Asperger's and Me", gave Connor a real sense of being like someone else. I recorded the programme and at a suitable time I suggested that he might like to watch it. We sat down together on the sofa and he spent much of the programme smiling and nodding at the situations that the presenter described.

With our increasing knowledge of autism and its characteristics, it would be fair to say that we knew Stephen was autistic long before any formal assessment took place. I think that his paediatrician felt the same way. We had discussed the possibility when he was quite young but had decided together not to pursue a diagnosis until the time was right. When he was placed with us for adoption we were aware that he was developmentally delayed due to his start in life if nothing else. As a result, he had been well supported in the school setting to date and the need for an official diagnosis of autism was not an urgent issue.

It is only recently that both Stephen and Harry have been diagnosed with autism. Both boys were referred to the ASCA pathway at the same time. I had heard that the waiting list for assessment had increased dramatically since Connor's diagnosis. With Stephen heading through primary school, I wanted to make sure he had an official diagnosis before any plans for transition to secondary school were in place. And it all started again. Form filling, report writing, visits from all the relevant professional services, just as it had for Connor a few years previously.

Dr Zoe Claisse has looked after Stephen in her capacity as a community paediatrician since before we had him. She knows Stephen very well and he adores her. I hope she doesn't mind me saying, but at every appointment I sit there thinking that she looks just like Professor Sprout from the "Harry Potter" films. It always brings me a little inner smile. I trust her judgement completely and I always leave an appointment with greater knowledge than I had before. We both agreed that it would be good to have an autism diagnosis for Stephen well before any decisions were made for his secondary school transition.

Harry's referral to the ASCA pathway came from a slightly different perspective. Harry has foetal alcohol syndrome (FAS), which I will come to later in this chapter, but with it he has autistic traits which needed further investigation. The paediatrician who had diagnosed the condition was very keen that autism be investigated. With Dr Claisse knowing both boys, she headed up both diagnostic pathways.

The day came again. The day for the diagnostic meeting. By this point we had a great deal more knowledge of autism and of the other conditions that both Stephen and Harry had already been diagnosed with. So, in a strange and slightly matter-of-fact way, waiting outside the room to be called in for the verdict was a less daunting prospect than you would imagine.

It was just me this time. In the room was the head teacher, Dr Claisse and the clinical psychologist, whom I had met before in a different capacity. After the usual niceties of welcoming me, Zoe asked me what I was expecting to hear. I said that I had no doubt that Stephen would receive an autistic spectrum diagnosis there and then, but that Harry was more complicated and that I was unsure whether he would be considered autistic. Zoe smiled and said I was completely right. The meeting unanimously agreed that Stephen had autism and that this was now confirmed in a formal diagnosis. Harry was more complicated.

He certainly had autistic traits, but it was felt that these were complicated by the FAS. In cases where it is unclear at the ASCA pathway assessment, referral is made to what is called the "third tier". Having said all that, the two people who would then decide based on reports and any further review were sitting in the room: Zoe and the clinical psychologist. Given that they both knew Harry and his background and were totally familiar with the reports, they agreed that should his case go to the third tier, they would both confirm autistic spectrum disorder. In short, they covered both levels of diagnosis in one. So that was it, three children with autism. Certainly, at different points on the "spectrum", but nevertheless all autistic. It was in many ways expected, but it was still a blow.

Steve and I sat having dinner that evening, almost in silence. It was like being in shock, but that wouldn't be the right word. In our hearts we knew Stephen was autistic, but I think we always hoped that Harry was the "normal" one. That word again. But I am sure you understand what I mean. We embarked on the adoption process to have a family, at no point during that process would we have imagined a few years later we would have three boys all with a diagnosis of autism, let alone all the problems associated with the condition and their other difficulties. During the adoption process, you go through a list of conditions or disabilities that you feel you would be able to cope with or accept. I do remember saying that we would accept minor learning disabilities, but I am sure we said no to autism. Thinking back to that day, two social workers sitting in our lounge with a checklist, reading out various difficulties and disabilities and asking us whether we would accept a child with such conditions. It was for us, and I am sure is for many prospective adopters, impossible to understand the real impact of parenting a child with any form of disability or difficulty based only on a list of named conditions.

By the time Stephen and Harry were both diagnosed, we were more than familiar with the challenges of living with autism, not only for the child with the condition but for us as their parents. The challenges that we face daily are significant. Even just getting the children to school each morning and then collecting them in the afternoons has been and continues to be something that presents greater difficulties than parenting neuro-typical children. All our children are affected by autism in different ways. It is understanding how their conditions affect their behaviour that gives us a greater chance of getting our parenting right. For example, Connor's thinking is particularly rigid and inflexible. Once he has a thought, an idea or a point of view on a subject, he is very unlikely to change. Meeting that with rigid and inflexible thinking on our part will not help matters at all. Of course, that does not mean simply giving in as parents, it is working through those issues in a more creative way that becomes the challenge for us. As you would imagine, we have learned this by making mistakes, many of them of a nature that has caused both Connor and us great distress, some of which I will come to later in Chapter 4.

To give you a simple example, travelling as a family is particularly difficult. As we know, social interaction is challenging and just getting in a car, sitting so closely to others, can cause difficulties. We have learned over the years that taking two cars rather than one gives us more space and less chance of a problem occurring between the boys. It also gives us an escape route. For example, our dearest friends and godparents to all three boys invited us over at Christmas time to join their family for drinks and supper. We knew that it would be socially rather a busy occasion, so putting our plan in place we took two cars. We had been there only half an hour or so when it was apparent that Connor was not coping. It was, however, in some ways a real breakthrough as Connor came to me and said he wanted to go home. It was serious, I could see that this was not simply a case of going home because he didn't want to be there, this was more like, I need to get out of here quickly. Christmas is such a difficult time of the year anyway, all those extra things around, decorations, lights, noise, it's just so much to cope with. So, if plan A was going as a family, plan B was activated and the escape route of having two cars gave Steve the opportunity to take Connor away. Stephen and Harry were able to enjoy the attention of their godparents without seeing their brother become stressed and anxious.

Well, that explains everything

In May 2012, having received the diagnosis that Connor was autistic, it just seemed that it explained everything. Of course, it certainly did not, but at the time we were so desperate for answers that having autism was the reason for everything. We had been Connor's parents for nearly six years, most of which was spent saying, "It's because he's adopted." That now changed to, "It's because he's autistic." He was then coming to the end of his third year of school, and in many ways we thought that having the diagnosis was the solution to our problems. The teachers would now treat him differently, educate him understanding his differences, and we would no longer be called in to school virtually every day to discuss his behaviour. That was so far from the truth of it. Things didn't really change. His teacher was wonderful, she was after all the teacher who had identified his behaviour as autistic rather than naughty, but she was just one probationer in an education system that was struggling to support children like Connor.

Break times and lunchtimes continued to be problematic, even going outside to play was difficult. Other children played games that Connor simply did not play or did not understand. So that meant he would dig in the dirt at the edge of the playing field while the other children would be playing football. He was promised a sandpit by the head teacher if he was "good". That was torture for him. He tried so hard to conform in order to get a sandpit. After a considerable period, the sandpit arrived – it was the smallest sandpit I had ever seen, and to make things worse he was then told it wasn't only for him, it was for the whole school. He had to share. Sharing has always been a real problem for Connor, as it has for Stephen and Harry.

Connor moved from playing in the dirt to playing in the sandpit, but other children wanted to play in it as well and there simply wasn't space. Difficulties arose, as you would imagine, and then the sandpit was taken away as Connor was "naughty". I was tearing my hair out – why didn't they understand? I had read the information provided in the pack and had started to access any form of information I could find on autism and Asperger's syndrome to help me understand my son better. I was almost shouting out, "He's not naughty, he's autistic."

Developmental delay and learning disability

When Stephen was placed with us for adoption we had been told that his development had been delayed due to his start in life. After all, how could a baby develop properly if he was left unaccompanied in a room, just strapped into a buggy? His foster carer saw the potential in Stephen and was very confident that he would catch up.

I am not sure what it means to simply be labelled as having developmental delay. It is so wide a description that it could really mean anything. Essentially, we always thought of Stephen as missing out on a start in life and that his life really began from when he was taken into care. Does that mean then that he is a year behind every other child of the same age? There is no clear answer to the question. He was cute as anything, but he would get upset at the smallest little thing. He was two years and three months old when he moved to us.

What experience did we really have of knowing when a child is delayed in his development? Connor had been with us just over two years. He was not yet four years old when Stephen was placed with us. Two children under four years of age and no knowledge or inkling of the difficulties that the boys would subsequently be diagnosed with.

By the time Stephen started school it was clear that he had not caught up with his peers. I met Mrs Harley, his pupil support assistant, in the supermarket the other evening. She was so fond of Stephen, and still is. He relied on her totally in his first year at school. We talked about the book and the story of the children, our family and how we all came to be together. She said, "Make sure you spell my name correctly."

As Stephen's time in primary school progressed, it became more and more evident that he was not able to keep up with children of a similar age, both academically and in the playground. Even though he was held back a year after primary one, he started to fall behind considerably in his learning development.

A learning disability was suggested as a possibility when Stephen was young but was not something that could be determined at that time. It was complicated by the neglect in that first year of his life. Eventually, when Stephen was around the age of 10, the school's learning support teacher was asked to assess him for dyslexia. The outcome of the assessment suggested that it was possible that he was severely dyslexic, but it was so difficult to perform the assessment as Stephen finds it so hard to concentrate and was unable to read anything. His spoken word is pretty good (provided it is on his preferred subject) so the chances are that he is severely dyslexic.

Around the same time, it was agreed that a cognitive assessment should be carried out to see where he was relevant to his peers. A lovely clinical psychologist from CAMHS carried out the assessment. It was in two parts, just a couple of weeks apart. I sat with Stephen while he was trying to do all the tests. He tried so hard, I was very proud of him. But as I sat there it was so obvious that the result would be a learning disability. At one point he held his head in his hands and said it hurt.

The result of the cognitive assessment came through as around two-and-a-half years delayed at that age. About right, I would say. Stephen then had another label, "learning disabled". It does not change anything, but it does provide a formal picture of him going forward and for the support that he may need at secondary school and later in life.

Stephen may be learning disabled, but he is still our only child to answer questions before the students on the television programme "University Challenge". The questions were clearly in his area of expertise, dinosaurs and sharks.

Attention deficit hyperactivity disorder

I am not sure whether I knew very much about attention deficit hyperactivity disorder, or ADHD as it is so commonly referred to, before the condition was even suggested to us. I had heard the term on many occasions and presumed that it was what it said on the tin: inattentiveness, hyperactivity and general impulsivity. If I am to be honest, I had always thought that people said it because their child was unmanageable or difficult to control. I now know so much more about the condition than I ever did before. With two of our children having a formal diagnosis of ADHD, Stephen and Harry, we manage their behavioural symptoms in the full knowledge that it is not their fault (well, mostly not their fault).

According to the NHS website,[4] the exact cause of ADHD is unknown but in some cases it can be genetic. Given the fact that our children are adopted, and that Stephen and Harry are not related genetically, this is an unknown for us. However, the website goes on to suggest three specific and plausible causes: (1) being born prematurely – as in Harry's case; (2) having a low birth weight – as with both Harry and Stephen; and (3) smoking, alcohol or drug abuse during pregnancy – there is some evidence of all three in both Harry and Stephen. From reading up on the condition, I know there are many suspected causes and much research has been carried out into why ADHD occurs.

The experts among you will discuss and look at detailed research of how and why ADHD can be caused and how the brain, particularly the frontal lobe, works in children and adults with the condition. However, it was once beautifully described to me as the brain having a four-stage process that simply does not work properly in people with ADHD. To give you the example that was given to me, I go to pick up a glass off the table, (a) my brain decides I would like a drink, (b) it considers how this will happen, (c) my hand goes forward, picks up the glass and brings it to my mouth, (d) the result is that I have now taken a sip of the drink. For children with ADHD, part (b) is omitted. The child decides to have a drink, hand immediately goes forward to pick up the glass and whoops, it all ends up on the floor.

4 NHS (National Health Service) (2016) Attention deficit hyperactivity disorder. Available at www.nhs.uk/conditions/attention-deficit-hyperactivity-disorder-adhd/, accessed 30 January 2018.

When Dr Claisse put this to me at one of Stephen's appointments, I could not stop laughing. It described Stephen perfectly.

Stephen was in primary two at the time, in his third year of school as he repeated primary one for many reasons, but particularly due to his developmental delay. He had started to become quite tricky to manage, not for any bad reason, but he was literally "all over the place". He climbed on everything in the house, could not sit down for any time at all, showed lack of focus in just about everything, and more. Taking him out of the house for anything was demanding and potentially dangerous, particularly with roads and car parks. At that time, it would be fair for me to admit that I didn't think his teacher was putting in good enough strategies or that he was supported well enough in class. She came out to see me one evening after school and said that she intended to speak to the head teacher about Stephen as she couldn't really manage him in class.

On reflection, it was the most honest and brave thing that any teacher could have done. We had a review appointment booked with Dr Claisse, and the teacher's honesty created an opportunity for Stephen to gain access to the "additional support class", effectively a class that specialised in children with additional needs. The class was in Stephen's school, although it was not only for children from that particular school.

I remember so well taking Stephen in to see Zoe. He was literally climbing the walls. The appointment was scheduled for the usual 45 minutes to an hour. After five minutes or so Zoe placed her pen on the table, looked at Stephen and said, "I think he has ADHD." He was six-and-a-half years old, he was and still is gorgeous, but he was quite simply everywhere. He had climbed onto the couch and was jumping up and down; he then headed to a table, then the chairs, then the height measure. We sat and watched him. No doubt in Zoe's mind that this was ADHD. But she was not allowed to diagnose such a condition based on just one appointment or observation. Now I was confused. His behaviour in the hospital for that appointment was the same as it was at home and as it was at school, yet a diagnosis could not be confirmed. Without a diagnosis, medication could not be offered or tried, so it was home again with only a glimmer of a solution on the horizon.

To diagnose ADHD, according to information provided by the NHS, certain criteria must be met, including symptoms being displayed for at least six months and starting before the age of 12; they must be present in at least two settings, so at home and at school, for example; they make life considerably more difficult than it would otherwise be; and lastly, they should not be a result of another condition or developmental delay.

The form filling started all over again. Forms were sent to us and to Stephen's school. Reports to be written by the school and all to be sent back to Zoe for analysis. By the next appointment I thought we were all set for a diagnosis, and with any luck some medication to help Stephen regulate the behavioural symptoms that had continued to present themselves. If only this were the case. Zoe's secretary had not received the forms back from the school, despite the head teacher's assurance that the forms and the report had been sent in well ahead of time. It all had to be done again as the photocopies kept on file at the school were not acceptable, the originals had to be submitted. More waiting and hoping for some medical intervention to help us manage.

By the next appointment, several more weeks down the line, the forms had been completed again and received. Unsurprisingly, the scoring system confirmed that the behavioural symptoms of ADHD were present in both home and school settings. A formal diagnosis of ADHD was given. So now it came to whether we would like to try some medication to help manage the symptoms. Zoe took me through the various options, what in her experience had worked well in others and the pros and cons of the various medications. So off we went with a prescription for a form of medication to effectively stimulate the brain into processing those four stages that I mentioned above. It was certainly not a magic cure; the medication took time to get into Stephen's system and it was difficult to tell at the start whether it was having an effect.

Harry was around the same age that Stephen had been – he had recently started primary three – when we really started to notice his behaviour deteriorating. I remember in primary two, a very experienced teacher used a few strategies to keep him engaged, and I wondered then what was ahead of us. By the time he was six and had started primary three, symptoms similar to Stephen's started to show themselves. When one child has already been diagnosed, it is so much easier to see it coming in another. Our GP was more than happy to make a referral and by our request it was off to see Zoe with our youngest child.

Living with ADHD in a family is challenging and tiring. While we have a collection of pets including four dogs, a few years ago we had a wonderful black Labrador called Jess. Jess would never sit still, she liked to walk round and round the living room when Steve and I were sitting down, it was exhausting watching her.

It is an analogy I make to watching either Stephen or Harry without medication. In the mornings or later in the evenings when their medication has worn off, just continuous movement, and in Stephen's case jumping up and down while talking at us – "at us" rather than "to us".

Both boys also found their ADHD symptoms exhausting. Both have become more aware of when they have had medication and when that medication is wearing off, which is quite a breakthrough and shows a growing maturity in their understanding.

With autism diagnosed in all three and ADHD in both Stephen and Harry, the mornings and evenings can be more than a tricky affair. Connor particularly is not a morning person, although he thinks he is. If he arrives in the kitchen with Harry jumping around not focusing on eating or dressing, then the situation can become volatile very quickly. For most parents, mornings are tricky. Just getting kids ready to go out of the house to school is challenging, but it takes every ounce of planning to ensure that we all leave the house on time and safely every morning. Routines are essential and any break in a routine or change of habit requires a new strategy or the next plan to be brought into operation. I think we should all receive a medal for simply arriving at school or at work on time on any day that we manage to do so. And we do manage. There have been times when that has seriously been in doubt, but now, touch wood and any other good luck charm going, we are managing.

Foetal alcohol syndrome

After a bit of a wait, the appointment for Harry to see Dr Claisse came around. I sat in the room with Harry climbing on the usual obstacles you see in a medical consultation room: the couch, chairs and tables. I chatted with Zoe, explained my concerns about Harry's hyperactivity and lack of focus, and said that I suspected he also had ADHD. She observed Harry as she had Stephen, but then called him over to sit down in front of her, which he did quite amicably. She was looking at his eyes, his mouth and the area in between his mouth and nose. I was confused. After a few moments she turned to me and said, "I think there are signs of foetal alcohol syndrome."

It was like a bolt out of the blue. I had heard the term on the preparation course that we attended during the time we were being assessed to adopt, but this was the first mention of the possibility in Harry. He was six-and-a-half years old. I remember the course referring to children with smaller heads and characteristic eyes but that was about it, I did not remember anything else.

Zoe explained, very much in layman's terms, that the sole cause of FAS is alcohol consumed during pregnancy. That it very much depended on when the alcohol was consumed as to the effect the consumption would have on the development of the unborn foetus and subsequent damage to the child's brain development. Effectively, that FAS is a brain injury caused prior to birth.

Zoe was looking at Harry's smooth philtrum, the area between his nose and his mouth, his flat nasal bridge, thin upper lip and his eyes being small and wide. Apparently, all these features led her to consider the condition. We talked about the possibility and whether alcohol consumed during pregnancy had been suspected or known. I sat there in the room, a little dazed, but thinking back to the information we received prior to adopting Harry. No, there was certainly no indication of a potential issue in the information we received or in any report or document that I could recall.

We had little information about Harry anyway. If you recall from Chapter 1, he ended up with surgery to correct an inguinal hernia shortly after he was placed with us for adoption. That suspected problem had not been mentioned to us. There was certainly no information on his health prior to birth. As the physical characteristics were described, I kept thinking of Harry at 11 months old. I look back now at a photograph we took of him during the time of introductions, the facial features were certainly there.

I was expecting to start the diagnostic process to determine whether Harry had ADHD, now I was looking at something quite different. But what did it all mean? There are several symptoms of the condition for which there is no cure according to the NHS website,[5] but one that was very specific to Harry: "mood, attention or behavioural problems – such as autism-like behaviour or attention deficit hyperactivity disorder (ADHD)."

The question was, did Harry have foetal alcohol syndrome? The only way to have a confirmed diagnosis, according to a colleague of Zoe's, a community paediatrician with a specialist interest in the condition, was to confirm that the mother had drunk alcohol during the pregnancy. More time passed, and Harry was still all over the place and without any medication to help the symptoms he was displaying.

---

[5] NHS (National Health Service) (2017) Foetal Alcohol Syndrome. Available at www.nhs.uk/conditions/foetal-alcohol-syndrome/, accessed 30 January 2018.

Eventually, and after some detective work on the part of the medical profession, we received a confirmed diagnosis of FAS. Both we as parents and the school completed the relevant forms to look at the behaviours and whether they warranted a diagnosis of ADHD in addition to FAS. This all took quite a few months. All the time we continued to do our best to manage the behaviours Harry was displaying both at home and at school.

Around the time of the initial diagnosis of FAS, Harry's difficult behaviour at school had escalated. Early on in his third year I received a telephone call asking if I could come in as Harry was destroying the classroom. Honestly, how on earth could a six-year-old child destroy a classroom? When I arrived at the school he was on his own in the classroom and it was totally trashed. He was throwing everything he could find – tables, chairs, papers, books, anything and everything. I was horrified. How could this happen? He was just a little boy with a bit of hyperactivity and now he was in a total mess. The school had removed everyone, including the teachers, "for their safety". What about the safety of my child? Why had no one gone in and simply held him? I opened the classroom door, went straight over and held him in my arms. He was in a state of shock. I simply could not understand what had caused him to be in such a state.

Of course, now we know so much more about Harry, the conditions that he suffers from and how those conditions manifest themselves in the behaviours he displays when anxious and under a great deal of stress. But at the time, I was so confused. The head teacher, teachers and support staff came in after me and then tried to encourage Harry to help clear up. After a short while I made the decision that Harry just needed to get out of the school and be given a chance to calm in a much less stressful environment, at home.

Unfortunately, this became not an isolated incident. I still want to shout out "He's not naughty, he's autistic" at the top of my voice. I always use the term autism in such cases as the behaviours that are demonstrated probably come from that area of difficulty, even if Harry's autism may have originated from FAS. As autism has become a more known and accepted condition in recent years, those both connected and unconnected to the condition perhaps have a little more understanding of it than they do of FAS.

Living with FAS must be a rollercoaster of emotions for Harry. Adoption UK refers to a quote from the founder of the National Organisation for Foetal Alcohol Syndrome-UK (NOFAS-UK), describing children and adults with FAS as "being robbed of parts of their brain or their functioning".[6] What a terrible waste. Harry is lucky in many ways – he is not learning disabled, nor does he have problems with his heart, lungs, liver, kidneys or other organs, which has been seen to occur in people with FAS. He also has good vision and hearing. However, he struggles so much with regulating his emotions – he can be so happy one minute and so angry the next. At these times, just being with him and caring for him is exhausting, not knowing what is coming next. He is an articulate, athletic and engaging young

---

[6] Adoption UK (2017) Living with Foetal Alcohol Spectrum Disorders (FASD). Available at www.adoptionuk.org/resources/article/living-foetal-alcohol-spectrum-disorders-fasd, accessed 30 January 2018.

boy with all these emotions running through his body all the time.

Sensory processing

As many parents of an autistic child would do, we have researched the condition and most importantly which aspects of the characteristics of autism apply to our children. Looking back at their short lives to date, so often must their senses have played a part in their subsequent behaviour.

Many children (and adults) on the autistic spectrum have difficulties with over- or under-stimulation of senses. In all our children it is over-stimulation that is the cause of many issues that we face daily. Too much information simply leads to overload, resulting in stress levels increasing, becoming more and more anxious, and eventually resulting in a "meltdown". Changes to the environment in which they live, go to school or play can result in enhanced levels of stress and anxiety. As parents we have become more and more aware of the situations our children face; in fact, I caught myself hearing a sound the other day across a crowded shop that I certainly would not have done if Harry had not been with me. In effect, being aware of my surroundings in more detail means that I am more prepared and more creative in my management of any potential problem before it becomes one.

In the BBC programme in which Chris Packham talks about his autism and his senses, he describes his sensory input as everything rushing in at the same time. Just watching my children in a new environment or taking them out for a walk or shopping, their senses are clearly heightened, sending information to their brains at such a fast rate. It must be exhausting for them. In everyday life we find ourselves in situations where the children's senses are being bombarded with information – they may hold it together quite well at the time, but expect the reaction to come later.

Before Connor went to school or nursery, he went each week to the toddler group. It was just before Christmas, he would have just turned three years old. The group managed to get tickets to the "Singing Kettle Christmas Show". I thought it would be lovely, a show aimed at younger children, lots of singing and participation. How wrong could I be? We had been in the theatre a matter of minutes and Connor had his hands over his ears and was going into some sort of tantrum, but not quite a tantrum, if that makes sense. I could not understand him. After some attempts at trying to get him to behave like the other children, we headed for the exit and for the calmness of the café without others there. It was a long wait for the show to finish and I was so disappointed. I could not understand why my child was not like the other children, enjoying the experience, singing and dancing. I felt as though I had failed in some strange way. All the other mums were with their children enjoying an experience and we were not part of it. If only I had known what I know now, we would simply not have been there in the first place.

Of course, we tried again the next year; this time it was Steve and I taking the boys on a family outing. By then we had Stephen as well, so a four-year-old and a two-year-old, unbeknown to us both on the autistic spectrum, and in a theatre of sound and colour everywhere. We managed the first half, which was certainly an achievement in itself.

When Stephen was placed with us, just being with him was an experience. Looking back, his continual need to gain as much sensory information as possible must have been overwhelming. Head virtually in a flushing toilet, the sound, smell and touch of the water. Shopping was particularly challenging. Stephen needed to look, touch, smell and taste virtually anything he could in the shop. On one occasion (and probably many more), he managed to reach out from the trolley seat and grab a lone banana on the shelf. I watched him. He looked at it closely, held it to his nose and then rubbed the banana skin on his cheek. Thank goodness no one else was around to see him. There must have been an overwhelming desire to know much more about the banana than simply the fact that it was a banana.

Shopping is problematic with three young boys. Who in their right mind would take three neuro-typical children to a supermarket, let alone three with such heightened sensory awareness? But we did; well, we had to. Unless Granny was there to help, Steve would be at work and if we needed something then off we went. I would try my hardest to make do without going shopping, but sometimes it was just an unavoidable necessity. Stephen and Harry in a double trolley would invariably create some sort of kerfuffle. Connor would be touching absolutely everything and would become overwhelmed by the noises and visual displays. At this point we did not know anything about autism or the other difficulties the boys suffer from, so we kept going, kept dealing with each situation or problem as it arose. It was exhausting for us as well as them.

Once Connor was diagnosed with autism, well actually before that, during the assessment stage, we became more and more aware of situations that had occurred and were happening that involved a heightened sensory awareness. The behaviours he was demonstrating at school in squashing wet paper towels, or just standing for ages with his hands under a running tap. He started to not sleep in his bed but on the floor next to his bed, or even under it. Was he seeking out different feelings between a soft bed and a hard floor? Or did under the bed feel safer than being in the bed? In a busy shopping centre or out walking the dogs in a forest or on the beach, he would become agitated, stressed even – he must have been hearing sounds that we could not hear or did not pay attention to.

Connor continues to like to touch things in shops. He is sensitive to sounds, but this can depend on the type of sound or how he is feeling at the time. Harry is very sensitive to environments he is not familiar with, particularly those including sounds and smells. This makes going somewhere new difficult and challenging. For Stephen, just about everything can be a problem in his sensory world. Somehow, he is the one who is learning and has learned to handle things better. He knows that he does not like the noise level in cinemas and simply will not go. He would love to be able to see the latest films in his areas of interest but he is prepared to wait for them to come out on DVD. The Marvel range of films, *Jurassic World*, *Star Wars* films, he has had to wait for them all well after his friends have seen them because the whole sensory experience of a cinema is just too much. Many of the cinemas have autistic-friendly showings, but it's still too much. When Stephen gets his new DVD, he runs straight up to his bedroom and watches it with no sound whatsoever. He probably watches it that way at least three or four times before turning on the sound slightly. Visually he is so observant, so by the time he watches it with sound, he knows the plot and all the "scary" bits.

For both Connor and Harry, clothing is one of the biggest and most troublesome areas of day-to-day life. It has been a problem since before we knew about autism, about sensory processing, about how different feelings can affect the child. Connor has always struggled with clothing, with finding something to wear that feels acceptable. But for both boys it is shoes and socks that are the most difficult. We have, in the past, simply not been able to leave the house as Connor could not find a pair of socks that felt comfortable. He could not leave the house without socks, nor could he put on a pair of socks. On one occasion he had a three-hour meltdown about socks during which he sat on the stool by the front door wanting to go out but unable to do so. He has an unusually wide foot and his little toes curl under in a way that is very uncomfortable. I have seen him screaming at me to have his toes amputated.

Harry has a similar-shaped foot and the same difficulties with both shoes and socks. I buy so many pairs of shoes and as Steve would put it, we are sock millionaires. Even now, with all the strategies in the world, getting out of the house in the mornings is nothing short of a miracle. When Harry will put on his socks and shoes without any moaning or fuss, it's an exceptionally good day. I get in the car with a smile on my face, a good start to the morning.

With three boys you would think that our house is a noisy and busy affair. But that could not be further from the truth. Our boys like to be quiet and to have their own space. The house is rather quiet most of the time. Televisions and computer console games might well be on, but they are at such a low level that everyone is happy. It is not always like this, but mostly it is a quiet and safe environment for the children to be as comfortable as possible. But being aware of what works and does not work in terms of noise, sound and smell particularly is something we have learned, and continue to learn, making many mistakes along the way.

Attachment disorder

From the time Stephen was placed with us for adoption, he was under the care of a community paediatrician, the wonderful Dr Claisse. As far back as I can remember, each time we had an appointment and visited Zoe, she would write a letter about the visit to our GP and copy Steve and I into the correspondence. The format was always the same: "Dear Dr…, I was pleased to see Stephen and his mum in clinic today…" At the top of the letter she nearly always listed the diagnosed conditions or possible conditions, depending on where we were with suspected or confirmed diagnosis.

Every so often one of the conditions would be listed as "possible attachment disorder". It is something that we talked about or around on the most basic of levels, but not something that I understood or was particularly worried about in Stephen.

Having an adopted child or children, attachment disorder is a real possibility. From birth we develop a bond with the people who provide the most care for us. Usually, our parents. But of course, it can be different people, other family members or in the case of children in the care system and in care from birth, most likely foster carers.

Both Connor and Harry were with a foster carer from birth and until they were placed with us. They both bonded with their respective carers and I believe that they were both fortunate not to have been moved around in the care system prior to placement with us as their permanent family. Having said that, I do think it is possible that Harry had quite a few people who cared for him in the setting in which he was placed. I am not sure who the main carer was and whether this has had an effect on him.

Adopting a child means that any attachments formed between the care giver and the child must effectively be broken and reformed with the new adoptive parents and family. For the specialists among you, I am sure that there is a great deal of psychological research into the effects of breaking formed attachments, but as adoptive parents we must just do the best job we can at forming a bond with our new child. A part of the preparation course when we first applied to adopt covered this area. I remember the social workers describing situations where it took some time for the new parents to learn to both like and love their adopted child. I suppose there is an analogy to having a child naturally and taking time to form the bond, or even just learning to love them. But it is common in adoption for that to take a little longer, all the time knowing that as adoptive parents we need to work hard on helping the child form the attachment to us as their care giver.

Harry was placed with us around nine months after we had Stephen. It was a short time after this that Harry ended up in hospital for his hernia operation. It was an emergency admission and Steve was away at the time. Considering Stephen's background, we were still working on attachments and having to reassure him on a regular basis that we would not leave him. When I had to leave him with Granny and head off with Harry into Edinburgh, I had no idea how long I would be away. I kept saying, "Mummies always come back." It was three days later that I brought Harry home after his surgery and got back for Connor and Stephen. It certainly set us back with Stephen's attachment. He became so worried if we even left the room after that. Nowadays he still needs reassurance, but it is better. When we are out, and he is looking round, I often feel a hand holding my clothing just to make sure I am still there.

I have never been particularly concerned about any of our children and their attachments to us. In chatting with Zoe, we have so far concluded that any symptoms Stephen has displayed that may lead us to think that he has an attachment disorder have not been severe enough for us to concern ourselves with an official diagnosis. Just researching the types of symptoms that can be displayed in such children is a minefield. Many characteristics are so close to the behavioural characteristics of autism, such as poor eye contact, that it would be difficult to diagnose anyway. Stephen certainly does not have some of the more severe or difficult behaviours that are noted as being associated with attachment disorder, which I am sure that many adoptive families will have experienced.

Stephen is a very affectionate child to us as his parents. He looks to us for reassurance much of the time and he enjoys physical contact, hugs and cuddles, but always on his terms. His lovely group of friends at school understand him and let him give them a hug and show his affection for them. I cannot praise this group of children enough for their understanding and the friendship that they show to him. It is unusual for a child of 11 to go up to his friends and hug them, but they accept him for who he is and enjoy his company. It is at such times that I marvel at the ability of children to adapt to their surroundings and just accept people.

Chapter 4

SCHOOL LIFE AND HOME LIFE

Attending a mainstream school

During this chapter I hope to give you an understanding of our experiences of mainstream education for two of our children who have significant additional educational needs. Both Connor and Harry have been in mainstream throughout their primary school education. While Stephen started in mainstream with a pupil support assistant to help him, he moved into a class for children with additional needs at quite a young age. Stephen's time at school has certainly been less problematic overall than that experienced by our other boys.

School life has such a huge impact on home life, I always think of us as picking up the pieces at the end of each school day – although most of the time it is a real struggle to work out what or where the pieces are. We have tried pretty much everything, from going in and speaking to teachers to the more drastic action of moving schools. As a great friend of mine and a retired behavioural scientist once described to me, it is not challenging behaviour that our children have, it is behaviour that challenges the adults around them to provide the right level of support. It is our role as parents to get the people around our children to understand and embrace their differences.

As you know, Connor had difficulty at school from the start. The way in which he interacted, or perhaps better put did not interact, with the people around him meant that he was "odd". The move to a different school at the end of his primary one year did not bring the solutions we were so hoping for. Of course, at that stage we had no idea that he had autism. The eventual diagnosis also did not bring solutions to the situations we were facing as parents or to the environment in which he was being educated. The more we read up on the condition, the more we needed the school and the teachers to understand that Connor was not able to engage in the same way as other children, yet he was somehow expected to.

At one meeting Steve asked the teachers whether they would expect a child with one leg to run up and down stairs. So why on earth was Connor expected to work in groups or be in a loud and busy classroom? While the analogy was understood, autism is often a hidden disability, and teachers forget the problems the child has, resulting in not seeing the warning signs before an incident occurs.

It was shortly after lunch on a summer's day. I was at home with Stephen and Harry, having picked them up from nursery. The phone rang. I could see from the number that it was the school. My heart sank, as it always did. I answered the call and it was the head teacher saying that there had been an incident in the playground at lunchtime. She said, "Connor has hit another boy on the head with a rock. We do not think the injury is life-threatening but the child has been taken to hospital." She asked me to go in and collect Connor as he was now excluded. I was devastated; what on earth had happened? What if the child's injuries had been life-threatening? What would that have meant for us and for Connor? A million things were rushing through my head.

My mum, bless her, came over and looked after Stephen and Harry while I rushed to the school. I was met at the door by the head teacher and told to take Connor home. She would discuss matters with me tomorrow. Connor looked awful. He sat in the car and said nothing. By the time I got him home he was just about able to speak. After a little while he told me that the other child had been hitting him with a stick and that he had picked up a stone and thrown it at him. That was certainly a different account than the one I had received earlier. Quite frankly, Connor couldn't hit a barn door from a yard, so managing to throw a stone that hit someone on the head was just a lucky or unlucky shot.

I took off Connor's clothes looking for evidence and found a terrible bruise on his arm, the shape of a stick across his upper arm. There was a similar bruise at the top of his forehead, on his hairline. I took photographs of the injuries.

By the time I met with the head teacher the next day, the injured child had returned to school with a small cut on his head that had been seen to at the hospital. Certainly not the dramatic and potentially life-threatening injury that had been indicated. In addition, several of the parents had already been into school as their children had corroborated Connor's account that the boy had been beating Connor with a stick. Connor's action of throwing the stone had come from what was happening to him rather than being a malicious and unprovoked attack. Suddenly, it was all brushed under the carpet, and Connor was not excluded. But there was no apology or acknowledgement of the supervision, or even the protection of, a vulnerable child.

Connor continued to have difficulties and he remained at that school for a period of just over two years before we moved him, on the advice of the Education Officer, to a larger school in St Andrews. I remember so well his first day at his third primary school. Stephen had moved on the same day into the primary one class, Connor into primary four. When I arrived to pick them up, Connor was in the corner of the classroom under a table. That sinking feeling again, and this was only the first day.

After being called in to talk to the teacher and deputy head, things did get a great deal better. The teacher had experience of autism in the classroom and in just a few weeks Connor settled and was managing some of the class activities. It was a great relief.

A few weeks before the end of term came the school show. Anyone from primary four to primary seven could audition for a part. Connor obviously did not put his name forward. But talking at home we found he was interested, he simply did not know what an audition was. By that time all the parts were taken but the teacher managed to get him in the cast for the understudies' performance. I could not believe my eyes – there was my son up on stage performing in a school show. The teacher came running after me that evening with tears in her eyes, "Mrs Otto, Mrs Otto, didn't he do well." She just understood.

Primary five was uneventful. The teacher managed Connor relatively well, she was precise in her instructions and her classroom was neat, tidy and generally quiet. All things that would work well for Connor. By primary six, life became very different. Connor was struggling with changing teachers again, a busy and messy classroom, changing tables around on a regular basis and an inconsistent approach. He spent nearly every afternoon barricaded in the sports cupboard just off the main hall. It was simply all too much. He was not coping with mainstream education, had no support in the classroom and was struggling with just being at school. It was almost as though autism was taking him over. He was failing to interact with other children in an appropriate and "normal" manner and was unable to express his feelings to the adults around him. There were so many occasions when I was called into the school to discuss his behaviour. One time the class teacher said, "If he was my child I would take him to a GP because he's not normal."

By the end of primary six the teacher had none of Connor's work to show, he had torn up every jotter or piece of work he had attempted. He was, quite frankly, in a state of crisis. We contemplated home schooling, changing schools again or even moving into the private sector. We looked at specialist schools for autism, but all possible options required local authority support and funding. Nothing seemed to be the right thing to do. We wrote to the Education Officer and she asked to meet us. Acknowledging the failings of the system in Connor's case, they offered to provide a pupil support assistant for Connor for primary seven, his last year at primary school. It was a level of support that he had not had before and a commitment that we certainly could not and would not turn down.

Due to the inevitable delays in employing the right person for the position, Connor started primary seven in the same state as primary six – he was unsettled and unable to cope with the school setting. However, a pupil support assistant was appointed and his school life changed for the better. He spent much of his time out of the classroom in a quieter setting, and much of it out and about looking at places in St Andrews and being educated by the PSA. By the end of primary seven he had jotters with work in, maybe not quite to the curriculum that was specified by the education authority, but it was a start and a good one at that. It just took more than six years of school life before the right level of support was provided.

Harry managed through the first couple of years of primary school quite well. He was the "normal" one, or so we thought. It was primary three when Harry's behaviour started to escalate to a level where he was not able to cope in a classroom setting. He was increasingly losing his temper and showing an inability to regulate his emotions. There were clear indications of ADHD and autistic traits, but he was still expected to behave in a classroom setting. It was like déjà vu. Having experienced such an emotional rollercoaster with Connor, I was not sure we would be strong enough to cope with another child having similar problems without support in the classroom.

From one school to another

When things go wrong for a child at school it is we parents who must somehow pick up the pieces. Whether you have a young child not wanting to leave their parents at the school gates or a teenager who is finding friendships tricky, we do our best to be there for them.

I am not sure we really discussed where Connor would start his school life; we just followed the neighbours in sending him to the same school as their young son. Of course, we did not know the difficulties that Connor had at the time and it seemed a sensible choice, by all accounts a lovely school with local children from the village and surrounding area, quite a few farming families, and Connor did love all the farm machinery that he saw daily from our windows and driving around in the car.

At the end of his first year, when it became evident that Connor had been bullied, we moved schools. A new start, everything would be much better. Only two classes in this school, mixed age groups and a real sense of a local community. But as you know, school life just became harder and harder for Connor. He used to get ready for school without a fuss, but once we were in the playground and the bell went, I needed help from the staff to peel my son off me on numerous occasions. It was soul destroying. Why was he not like the other children? What were we doing wrong?

Of course, it was at this second school that he was diagnosed as autistic. But it did not change anything for Connor. Autism is not a curable disease. It is a condition or disorder that means that my child thinks and acts in a different manner than a person who could be described as neuro-typical. There is so much known about the condition and, particularly in a school setting, strategies that can make the child feel more comfortable, happier. Is it the child or is it the school that is the problem?

A further change of primary school became necessary during Stephen's second year of school life. We had hoped that Stephen would have had access to the additional support class at this time, but the paperwork had not been submitted correctly. We decided to go for the change of school; it must be the school that is the problem. Connor had been at school for three and a half years and we were now on our third school in search of the care and support our children needed.

Still to this day I am not convinced we made good decisions about where our children were educated at the primary stage. Yet I have also not come across a school that I can see our children fitting in to. I often wonder whether we were right to change schools in search of the solution to our problems. But we tried. Making the decision to change your child's world, whether they have diagnosed difficulties or not, is such a massive decision to make. Looking back, we should have researched all the options more thoroughly. We may still have moved the children and to the schools that they have been at, but one thing that I have learned along the way is that the more knowledge we have, the better decisions we can make.

The impact of school life on home life

From the start of primary one for Connor, school had such an impact on home life. I recall the discussions at toddler groups and when taking or picking up the children from nursery that it all changes once the children go to school. How right they were, but for probably different reasons than for other families.

The day that Connor started school was also Stephen's first day at nursery. From then on simply going to and from school with three children was a military exercise.

And it still is. Merely getting everyone ready to arrive at school at the correct time is a challenge. It was evident from an early stage that school was impacting Connor's life and his life at home. He was a happy boy before he started school, but he lacked the ability to socialise in a similar way to the other children. As his first year progressed I was called in more and more to discuss his behaviour. I would then be upset and angry at him for not behaving, something that I so regret. We just did not know why.

In Stephen's second year at school, our beautiful and gentle little boy started to pick up some very poor language from a couple of the other children. Suddenly he was starting to say rude words at home, and I was really upset. Probably rather naively I did not expect my young child to be hearing such language at that age or at primary school. Stephen did not actually understand what he was saying, he could just see that it certainly got a reaction. I hated it. Eventually, after much explaining and many incidents, Stephen did start to understand that children must not say certain words.

The early years of primary school life were difficult, but the impact that school had on home life became more dramatic as the children began to show behaviours and symptoms of their conditions. For Connor, the trauma of shutting himself away from others by blockading himself in the gym cupboard every afternoon was so evident. He was quiet and withdrawn at home, taking out his frustrations on his brothers, whom he probably perceived to be having a much easier time. He really wanted friends, but they were not there. He would go on and on about going to someone's house to play, but he had not been invited.

The usual birthday party invitations came out, but only a very few came to Connor and that was only when the parents invited the whole class. He tried going but found the whole experience overwhelming. He did not like the loud noises, could not understand the point of party games, and sitting down to socialise over food was beyond his capabilities. We would try and then go. As time progressed, he was invited to fewer and fewer. Eventually none. He was the awkward child that did not really fit. Despite his desire to have friends and want to go to others' houses and have people back to ours, he was just not on the same wavelength as the other children.

Within the classroom he struggled. Being in a group for reading or for any work was so overwhelming that he would shut down. But despite being told on numerous occasions that work in groups was so difficult for Connor, the teachers persisted. Eventually the team from ASIST (Autism Support in Schools Team) came in to view him in class and give the teachers strategies to help him in the classroom. Connor does not have any difficulty in learning, just a slower processing speed than others, therefore he had to remain in mainstream education. There were no alternatives available. Every afternoon I would arrive at the school, collect the children and start to attempt to pick up the pieces of another traumatic day. Connor would be angry and aggressive to me and to his brothers, his way of reacting to the overwhelming experience of a school day.

By the time Harry was in primary three, things started to go wrong. He was clearly having similar problems with being in a mainstream classroom and whenever possible would head to the quiet of the school office to hide away from others. That was at least better than trashing the classroom, which has happened on numerous occasions.

Harry's stress and anxiety levels at the thought of going to school became more evident. Even on days when the teacher has said "It's been a good day", he has stood and kicked and hit his head on the wall on the way back to the car. With other children running past happy to be out of school, my child is hurting himself and on purpose.

By the time we arrived home, it would take every ounce of my energy to manage the children, to try to settle them and repair the effects of school life.

As you can tell, it is Connor and Harry who are most affected, both in mainstream classes. Stephen has always been relatively happy at school, particularly once he was placed in the class for additional support, or special needs as I tend to refer to it. He has, however, been as much affected by Connor and Harry's experience as they have. He has seen them distraught, angry and upset on many occasions. For all his difficulties, he knows when to hide away from the situation, immersing himself in a jigsaw puzzle or computer game or playing on his iPad, while I attempt to pick up the pieces of the day.

Having been through some extremely difficult times with Connor, Harry has benefited slightly from Steve and I having a greater understanding gained from Connor's experience of mainstream education. We are both capable individuals who are not afraid of challenging a situation if we feel it is necessary. With Harry becoming more and more anxious in school and his behaviour becoming more and more challenging, a meeting was called to discuss what support was available.

I remember sitting in a room in the school with the head teacher, educational psychologist, class teacher and a member of the team from the specialist school for pupil support (which deals with children with challenges that are not being met in a mainstream setting). The meeting started and the representative from pupil support opened by saying that Harry would be a lower priority for support as their remit was to help "looked-after children". In other words, children in the care system. My reaction was quite assertive as I asked for clarification as to why my adopted child was a lower priority for the education authority than if I were fostering. I clarified that if that was the case, it would be something that I would be taking further. It seemed to be the right stance. Support was more forthcoming, Harry would be helped by their service. In fact, for a few months he went off in a taxi to the pupil support school three afternoons a week. It took time, but it helped. He is back in mainstream school and while life is not perfect by any means, and after school we continue to struggle, it is better.

Connor is now at secondary school. Having heard about the experiences of his primary education from us and from the primary school in its report, the school moved Connor out of mainstream and into a special class called the "On Course Centre" for the first year of his secondary education. What a difference this has made to him and to our life at home as a result. He had an extensive transitional period during his last year at primary school and starting on his first day was absolutely no problem.

A few weeks after starting we were invited to parents' evening. Not an occasion I had ever looked forward to in the past; in fact, we were called in so often to discuss the children at primary school that I had stopped going to parents' evening. This time we both left the room in tears. Not tears of heartbreak as in the past, we were overwhelmed with pride, our son had found his place. He was working well and was enjoying school. The wonderful Mrs Scott had worked so hard on building up a relationship of trust with him that he was learning and engaging in the classroom. He is now in his second year and has, by his own request, started some mainstream classes. Another parents' evening, shortly after starting these new classes, and the teachers were all so complimentary: "Connor is amazing"; "Since joining the class Connor has changed the dynamic for the good"; "Connor works hard and is enjoying the subject." Every teacher had positive words. Connor was with us and was so proud.

Both Steve and I are more than aware that it will not always be like this, but it is a glimmer of hope, and a big one, not only that will Connor have every chance at reaching his potential, but that Stephen and Harry will be well supported in their secondary education when the time comes.

With school life getting better, life at home is better. The children are more settled when they arrive home. They will always need time to recover from whatever experiences the day has thrown at them, but the atmosphere is calmer and more "normal" than it has ever been before.

Activities after school

I watch the other parents rushing around after the school pick-up, off to roller hockey, football, judo, taekwondo, or Glee Club, to give a few examples. Of course, we tried some of them with our boys. For Connor every Saturday morning from the age of five (when it was evident that his behaviour was rather challenging at school) until the age of around nine, we drove him to and from his judo class. It was a short class, around 40 minutes. He managed. He even won the class trophy a few times during this period, and we were very proud. Unfortunately, it did not last beyond this age. He had achieved quite a few belts but had no desire to compete in the sport and I think he really went to spend time with either Steve or I, whoever was taking him that Saturday.

Connor's autistic behaviours became more significant around that age and he could not cope with people touching him. Of course, judo is a full-contact sport and not something that he could manage any longer.

He was not interested in any after-school activities – we tried art classes, pottery, swimming – but all eventually stopped as he no longer wanted to take part. If any had been just one to one then I think he would have liked to try, but not in groups and certainly no sports that involved physical contact.

Stephen went for a short time to a drama club, which he seemed to enjoy once he got to know the others there. Harry joined as well, but the people running the club were unable to cope with the needs of Stephen and Harry and therefore that had to stop. It was such a shame. Both children would have benefited greatly from such an activity but there was not the level of staff required to help them.

Harry started judo at a different club from Connor's, in a local hall. He loved it. But around the same time his ADHD symptoms started to manifest. He went a few times, but it was difficult for him to take direction and follow the instructions. The class was busy and loud. Not the environment for a child with Harry's significant needs. In the end I received a phone call from the instructor and owner of the club. He said he could not manage Harry in the class. He was clearly disappointed but explained that it was not financially viable for him to employ more people. Harry was upset at not being able to go. I was devastated.

When I think back to my childhood, at the age my boys are now I did not go to many organised activities. Brownies and then Guides, but that stopped as I was so keen on playing golf instead. Otherwise, I would be playing outside with my friends in the small cul-de-sac where we lived. Nowadays, there are so many clubs and activities for children, certainly for neuro-typical children. Unfortunately, we live rurally and, as such, the activities organised by autistic charities are a fair distance from us, simply not practicable for anything after school.

Having said that, children go to school for six to seven hours per day. That is a long time for the boys to socialise and interact with people. It is a long time for them to hold their concentration and be in a busy and sometimes loud environment. Coming home and settling down is an achievement. Having been through trying clubs and activities we are now comfortable that we are doing the right thing for our boys in not pushing them into such activities. Let them have time at the end of each day to recoup, relax and simply de-stress after the busy school day.

At some point in the future, we will try again. But not yet, not until they are ready or they show such an interest. In the meantime, I will sit back and watch the other parents as they pick children up, drop them off, pick them up again, and think that a life with autistic children can be calmer than that of the neuro-typical world.

When it all goes wrong, how wrong can it go?

This is probably the toughest part of the book to write. To tell you about how wrong it has gone for us in the past. As I write "in the past" I really do hope it is, but I would be foolish not to think that difficult times are still to come. After all, we have three boys with significant and very different needs. The oldest is only just a teenager. The younger two are still in primary school, so we have transitions to secondary school and their teenage years to come. Without doubt there will be heartbreak and tears, but I hope that we have learned enough, and continue to learn, about their difficulties to provide the support and nurturing environment that they need.

One of the most difficult things that we have done is to ask for help. By the time things started to go very wrong, we had tried our hardest to seek help and advice through schools, educational psychologists and the Child and Adolescent Mental Health Services. While we seemed to have a route into talking to people, there appeared to be no actual intervention available for our son. To say Connor was struggling is an understatement. By the age of 10 he was barricading himself in the gym cupboard at school every afternoon. School life was so disorganised and unstructured that it was having a terrible effect on home life. The Christmas after his tenth birthday, there were lots of presents under the tree. The boys had been given an extra bag of presents by a local charity that had provided Connor with a befriender (more of that in Chapter 5). It was just too much, with all the presents from Santa, from us and from family and friends, it was overwhelming. Connor tried to throw out all his presents that morning, he wanted to burn them all. After a five-and-a-half-hour autistic meltdown, he finally fell asleep on the sofa.

It is only looking back on the situation, the excitement of Christmas, the changes that Christmas time brings to an autistic family, that we can reflect and see where it went wrong. At the time it was simply a case of managing as best we could. I am not sure we did. It was a very tearful day.

Connor's autism is significant. I am often asked, "How bad are they?" If I can describe it the way it was once explained to me: autism is a spectrum, as most of you reading this will know. Where on the spectrum someone is does not give an indication of how their life is affected by autism. Connor's diagnosis is "very secure", in other words, for us and for him, life is significantly affected by his autism.

We managed our way through the rest of the Christmas break that year. All Connor's presents were hidden away as he was not able to accept any at that stage. It was an unsettled but expected start to the new year at school. Then his class teacher came up with the statement that made my heart sink: "We will give him until the end of January." What on earth did that mean? Give him until a certain date, then what? School life continued to be difficult. He was not coping, was not engaging, and it was having a serious and detrimental effect on our family.

We looked at moving to a new house but decided after much consideration and discussion to make some changes to our own house to help find space for everyone. Steve and I had found that we only had the kitchen in which to talk and spend time with each other, with the boys taking up the other rooms and all wanting their own space. The first and most obvious change was a loft extension. We discussed it at length with the boys and in particularly Connor. It would be Connor's room. After all the architect's plans and thoughts, it was Connor at 10 years old who came up with the solution for how it could be done. He was excited and happy to be getting a new room in the loft. It would be a much bigger space and he would have his own bathroom.

In appointing the builders, we stressed the importance of a quick turnaround for the work. Easier said than done. We knew that it would be difficult for Connor to see his existing room ripped apart and all the changes to the house, builders in and out the door. Each night as soon as the builders left I cleaned up as best I could to try to avoid stress levels getting too high. It didn't work.

Just after Connor's eleventh birthday, we had the worst night that we had ever had. Connor was stressed, as we were, with all the work being undertaken. Fortunately, both Stephen and Harry were in bed and asleep when Connor's stress levels went beyond boiling point. He started to melt down in such a way that we had never seen before. Things were being thrown and broken, he was pulling down curtains, smashing pictures, and there was nothing we could do to stop him. With Steve taking punches and trying his hardest to calm him, I phoned the clinical psychologist who had been helping us. By this time, this behaviour had already been going on for a considerable time. She said he would eventually calm but to call the police for help. We did. It was so traumatic for me, for Steve and for Connor. With Police Scotland now run centrally, it took a long time before anyone arrived to help. Connor was still in meltdown when they got there. He calmed immediately. This was the first of the vulnerable person's reports that would be submitted following an incident with the boys. It was devastating. At the centre of this was a young boy who was struggling with the environment around him and his parents who just needed help and support to understand him better.

The loft extension was finished a few days before Christmas, thank goodness. We went away to a holiday park the week before for a break, somewhere the boys knew well. This allowed the builders to completely move all their building materials out of the house. After all the disruption, the break was needed and was one of the best holidays we have ever had.

There have been other incidents, of course, some of which have involved us seeking further help from the police. Just going to and from school with three boys in the car in such proximity to each other is problematic. It is not that they do not care for each other, because they clearly do. It is that their stress and anxiety about the world about them creates a tension that is significantly more than would happen if they were not autistic. While going to school in the mornings was fraught, coming home was worse. After a day of social interaction and sensory overload, Connor and Harry would be at loggerheads over the smallest, and what anyone else would consider the most trivial, of things.

It was the January after the building work had been completed. Connor came out of school very stressed. I did not know why. But I had to call in and get prescriptions on the way home, not the usual routine. If I had realised how stressed he was, the prescriptions would have waited. He was hitting out at Harry in the car. It escalated to the point that he was physically uncontrollable and I had to stop the car. Connor grabbed the keys and threw them into a field. I had to get Stephen and Harry home, away from Connor. What a decision to have to make. To this day I do not think that I could have done anything else given the escalation. With Stephen and Harry safe and being cared for, I went back for Connor. The car had been smashed and kicked in the inside and Harry's iPad lay in pieces on the road. Connor had disappeared. I phoned for the police and then called Steve. It was getting dark and it was cold. Eventually, with police cars out looking for him, Steve found him in the middle of a field. Confused and unable to express himself.

Recently, I listened to a Radio 4 programme, "Adoption: Families in Crisis". I think we were there at that time. We were in crisis. I felt so much for the families talking about how adoption had changed their lives and how, in some cases, the adoptions had failed.

At that time, we were distraught. Our beautiful, talented and articulate child not coping with the world around him and taking it out on the people closest to him. The vulnerable persons report completed by the police must have highlighted the difficulties of travelling to and from school because as a result the local authority agreed, and quickly, to provide Connor with taxi transport. It was such a relief. That time between school and home was so difficult and we did not have a solution ourselves.

Obviously, a change of routine in getting in a taxi, and one that did not smell like our car, was difficult, but not as difficult as travelling together. It made such a huge difference to our lives. Connor was in his last year at primary school. He was just about to start an enhanced transition to secondary school, so taxi transport was "sold" to him as part of that transition and growing up. I think he missed me not driving him in a strange way. I think he missed being with his brothers, but it was simply not something he could do at that time.

With all incidents it takes Connor several weeks to settle, something to do with cortisol levels in the brain. However, it is like walking on eggshells until he is calmer and more settled. I often wonder how on earth he must feel during this time. It must be such a rollercoaster for him to ride.

The number of times Steve and I would sit there and ask ourselves if we could really do this – could we continue, and if not, what would that mean? We had no answers and no options, we just did our best to understand, to learn and to adapt our own behaviours to try to cope with not only Connor but our other two boys, Stephen and Harry.

A couple of years later, I sit here writing this book. Reflecting on that time and where we are now. Once Connor started secondary school things changed. The school placed him in the "On Course Centre", a nurturing class for children who cannot really cope either at all or at times with mainstream education. Life changed for Connor and for us. He loves school. He loves his teacher, the wonderful and talented Mrs Scott. Not only that, he has, at his own request, started some mainstream classes. It is without doubt the fact that this secondary school has been innovative in the type of education it can provide that our son is now a very different boy. He is still Connor, he still has significant autism, he is a teenager, but he is thriving. Every day is planned, every day is thought about and reflected on. Life is exhausting with three boys with autistic spectrum disorder, but we are getting there.

Educating teachers about my child

I vividly remember sitting in the head teacher's office at primary school and hearing the words, "We have other autistic children in this school and none of them are like Connor." I had no words. Surely every child is different? The fact that he is an individual and has very individual needs does not make him naughty. Steve saw a lovely tag line when looking through some information on autism: "Once you have met one child with autism, you have met one child with autism."

This was just one of many visits to the head teacher to discuss any one of my children. In this case it was Connor, but equally it could have been Stephen or Harry. In the case of behaviour issues that are regarded as naughty, it is certainly more likely to have been Connor or Harry; Stephen's one and only "naughty" behaviour was the karate chopping of the work on display in his first year of school.

For much of the children's first few years I dutifully went into school each afternoon that I was called in, pretty much every day, to listen to the teacher's comments on my son's behaviour. On some occasions the teachers were queuing up; which one should I talk to first? I had so little to offer in terms of how to change their behaviour to conform to that of the rest of the class. Even when Connor was diagnosed with autism I still had little to offer. I heard what the teachers were saying, he has done this or that, all of which were behaviours that I did not understand, but none of which I thought of as "naughty". Steve would be waiting at work for my call each day, dreading the fact that I had been called in yet again. As I reflect on this with the knowledge I have now, it is undoubtedly the environment in which they find themselves that creates the behaviour, not a wilful act on the part of the child.

Each year of Connor's primary school life, around the middle of September I would be told "We will give him until the end of term"; effectively this meant early to mid-October. I never did ask what would happen after that. One of the comedians on "Live at the Apollo" the other evening talked about parents and counting to their children. What would happen when they reached ten or counted back from ten and reached zero, nothing at all. It was just like that. Things were never better by the end of the first term, nor by Christmas, nor by half term, nor by Easter. And the pattern continued again the next year.

On many occasions I was asked what home life was like, as though there was a problem at home that was affecting my child's behaviour at school. Whether it was Steve away on business, Granny in hospital or one of the pets poorly, home life was then considered the contributory factor for the resulting behaviour of the children at school. In reality, it is at home that we pick up the pieces of school life. This is extremely difficult as our children are unable to explain what has happened during their school day – school is very separate from home and once out of the school gates they are unable to talk about it. If we have not been told, we attempt to piece together whether it has been a good day or a bad day from their body language, with no idea what has happened. From Connor coming out of school angry and aggressive, to Harry hitting his head on a wall in the school grounds, it is from this moment on that the rest of the day takes shape.

Since discovering that our children have the disabilities that they do, we have made every effort to understand those conditions and how they influence the way the children develop and behave. Like all parents, we know our children, how they feel, how they react, what makes them happy and what makes them sad. It is this knowledge of our children that gives us as parents the perfect platform to educate the teachers about them.

I have been in meetings with teachers, educational psychologists and the like and heard reference to these people as "The Professionals". I would sit there thinking that I must be the amateur in this. As parents we are also experts, we have a much greater knowledge of our children and as such we should be equal in assessing not only how our children's needs can be met but how the environment in which they are educated can be adapted to help them. For example, all our boys are particularly sensitive to sound. Harry's desk was next to a partitioned wall to the next classroom. In the adjacent classroom was a class practising their singing for the school show. Harry managed to say that he could not stand the noise, but the teacher did not react to his needs and left him at his desk. He quickly went into meltdown, started throwing things and the class was then evacuated. It left Harry on his own, deeply distressed and unable to function. He hit out at teachers and staff and tried to run away. When I was called in, the deputy head teacher went through the course of events and summarised by saying that Harry needed to tell them when he was feeling as though he was unable to cope. I asked her to read out again the first line of her notes: "Harry said he could not stand the noise." How clearer could he be? She then said, "Ah, we may not have reacted quickly enough." That evening we were left picking up the pieces of an avoidable situation.

It is imperative that the teaching and support staff in schools listen and adapt to the needs of the children they teach. It is only when parents and teachers work together that changes can be made. All the plans in the world, whatever names are given to them – integrated support plan, additional support plan, personal learning plan, etc. – they need to be effective and to be a plan for the child. On one occasion I refused to sign an integrated support plan document on the basis that it was simply a list of what my child could and could not do, not a plan for how my child would be educated around his specific needs. Parents and teachers should be in partnership to provide the right environment for children to learn. To quote Albert Einstein: "I never teach my pupils, I only provide the conditions in which they can learn."

Chapter 5

MEDICATION AND OTHER INTERVENTIONS

Can I make my child better?

With every effort to improve the situations we have faced, the question of whether we could make our child better has been at the forefront of our minds for a very long time. In this chapter I discuss this issue and the types of medication our children have to help them through daily life. It is, of course, not just medication but also other interventions such as psychology and befriending that offer support to a family in such circumstances.

When Connor was diagnosed with autistic spectrum disorder I rather naively thought that there would be some medication for him to take. I was not sure what it would be for or what I would have liked it to achieve, but I assumed that medication would be offered. Receiving the diagnosis and pack of information on autism, there was no suggestion of any follow-up appointment to discuss where we went from there. It was more like, there is the diagnosis and good luck to you.

We now know that there is no cure for autism. But the question is, would we or any of our boys cure their autism should it be possible? The BBC programme featuring Chris Packham, "Asperger's and Me", asked that very question. His response was at times yes, absolutely, but overall no, it would change him, he would not be himself. Steve and I talk about this now and again. Particularly when things have been so challenging that we have been in crisis as a family. It is such an interesting question. If there was a cure then the boys would not be themselves, with their special talents and interests. From Connor's current interest in engines and anything mechanical to Stephen's encyclopaedic knowledge of dinosaurs, sharks, some other animals and of course Marvel superheroes. Not forgetting Harry's depth of knowledge of World Wars I and II. His interest in military warfare and history. Three very different boys, all with autism. Overall, we come to the same conclusion as Chris Packham: at times yes, absolutely, take away the pain of autism. When I say pain, it is the pain of struggling with friendships, struggling with anxieties, that obsessive behaviour and rigid thinking and sensory processing that make life so difficult. But mostly, I would not change them for the world. They are three very special and amazing boys whom I hope will develop into young adults fulfilling whatever potential they have as individuals.

It is not just autistic spectrum disorder that two of our boys have, Stephen and Harry both suffer from ADHD, for which there is medication that can help alleviate the symptoms. From the moment that ADHD was suspected in both Stephen and Harry it took considerable time for an official diagnosis to be given. All that form filling and waiting for the results to be assessed, and of course, the next appointment. Once diagnosed the possibility of medication was discussed and offered. It is certainly not an exact science. I now understand that it really depends on what part of the brain is affected as to what medication will work best for that individual. It was and still is trial and error.

In both Stephen and Harry, the medication significantly affects their appetite. Stephen is small for his age and we do all we can to get as many calories into him as possible. As the wonderful Dr Claisse once said, "As much cake as possible and we will worry about his teeth later." Once the medication runs out, he eats and very much enjoys visiting the pantry and fridge of an evening. For Harry, the effect is much more problematic. Any meal or snack is met with refusal and possible aggression. The effect of not eating creates low blood sugar and challenging behaviour. He is anxious and has significant mood swings – just one bite can make all the difference, but he refuses. It is currently the most difficult of the behaviours that we are coping with and it is directly attributable to the medication. On a day that he does not take medication, he is hyperactive and has difficulty following instructions, but he eats and he sleeps. It is a real dilemma for us, to medicate or not to medicate.

Over the course of Connor's time at primary school, he suffered from anxieties that resulted in trying some medication to reduce those symptoms. It started relatively successfully but as the dosage increased it had a negative effect and may have made matters worse. We wanted him to try the smaller dose again but by this point he refused to take it, saying that he hated it and it made him feel awful. He refused to go into the appointment to see the child psychiatrist who had prescribed the medication and in the end we had to leave it. His thinking was rigid, and any discussion resulted in a meltdown that needed to be avoided.

Harry's behaviour at school was getting worse and worse at the stage at which we asked for medical intervention to help address his anxieties. Eventually we managed to get an appointment with the child psychiatrist Connor had seen. She is always so kind, always asks after Connor, and I think she somehow feels that she let Connor down. Harry has some medication to try to help reduce his anxious behaviour. It is the smallest of doses, but there was some correlation between starting this medication and improvements in how he was coping in a school setting. With Connor and Harry being genetically related, we have been extremely cautious over not increasing the dose until it is necessary to do so.

Medication is a changing playing field, it requires review and adjustment when necessary. It is something that we discuss so much, whether we are doing the right thing in medicating. For Stephen we are certain that the medication is effective and really helps him manage through each day. For Harry, we are not so sure. Currently, and on balance, it is the right thing to do, but this could change. He is complicated, he has FAS, ADHD and autism, life is tricky to say the least.

Like many children on the autistic spectrum or with other difficulties, sleeping is problematic, so they all have melatonin to help them get off to sleep and have a restful night. For both Connor and Harry, the medications that they have and in the current dose work perfectly. Without melatonin Connor would still be awake well after midnight each night. Stephen finds going to sleep the most difficult – without any form of medication to help him, he would be wide awake and hyperactive well into the night. As it is, the melatonin is not enough and he has what we call "knock-out drops" to finally get him off to sleep. It is something that we continue to struggle with each evening. Stephen is up and down, visiting the pantry and fridge as his ADHD medication has worn off, he is hungry and needs to eat. We often make him porridge or chicken burgers late at night to sustain his appetite. He needs calories and it is such a balance to allow him to eat late at night while also needing him to get to sleep. And then of course it is the dentist who then queries what types of food he is eating for the health of his teeth. I always think of dental visits as the bad-parent appointment. Continuously I have to justify eating patterns and explain about the supressed appetite with medication and how he then needs to eat late in the day.

There are medications out there to help with the symptoms of some of the conditions that the boys suffer with, in their case ADHD, anxieties and sleep disorders. Does it cure them? Certainly not, but it does help. It helps them to cope with life, to follow instructions at school and at home, to be less anxious about the world around them and, of course, to sleep, which is so essential for their health and well-being.

Psychology

Psychology, the scientific study of the mind and behaviour. Could this help my child behave in a more acceptable way? It was when Connor was just six years old that we sought some form of psychological help. At the time, this meant that Steve and I went to talk to two child psychotherapists about our son and the type of behaviours he was presenting and the difficulties we were experiencing, seeking to gain as much information as possible. While he was observed in his school setting, there was no direct intervention offered at this early stage. In fact, there was also no suggestion that the behaviours noted could be indications of autism.

I remember sitting in an appointment with Stephen to see Dr Claisse and the conversation moved on to our other children. I sat in her office nearly in tears as I started to talk about Connor's behaviour. She was wonderful and suggested that I ask our GP or Connor's community paediatrician for a referral to see a child psychiatrist friend of hers who she was sure would be able to help. Connor was seven-and-a-half years old.

Despite the referral, by the time he was nine we still had not managed to see anyone. Desperate for advice and intervention we approached a psychologist in private practice. It was through a recommendation, chatting to a friend with a young son about the same age. She had sought the advice of this psychologist and had very much liked her manner and respected her professionalism. I made contact and Steve and I went to see her. We talked in depth about Connor, Stephen and Harry. About Connor's behaviour at school and at home. She was wonderful. Herself the mother of three children, all with autistic spectrum disorder, she could not only provide a professional opinion, she had tremendous empathy for our situation.

Connor visited her after school; in fact, she even picked him up from school on the days of his appointments. In some ways it was a break for me, picking up two instead of three from school was a great deal easier and less stressful. He was happy to go. He liked her, he liked her dog, and he liked the wood-burning stove she had in the room. It was at least a place he enjoyed going and he was comfortable and relaxed. He was, however, very reluctant to talk about the difficult things in life.

The psychologist provided considerable advice to us, strategies that might help and make life a little easier. These ranged from visual timetables and schedules to providing clear and precise explanations of what was expected, when it would happen and how long it would last. Best of all was the idea of "social stories". In many ways this was the most effective of all the strategies suggested. For example, in the car coming home from a shopping trip, we start to talk to Connor about what is going to happen when he gets home, asking him what he will be doing and trying to find that direction for the next stage of the day. It is a simple but hugely beneficial strategy and one that we continue to use with effective results.

Of course, we do not always remember. The difference is huge. How well the children cope during each day relies on them knowing "The Plan". The plan of what is going to happen in the morning, at lunchtime, in the afternoon and in the evening. It is exhausting for us to manage to remember to keep referring to the social stories of each day. It is when the children are at their most anxious that it is imperative that we do remember and go back to this simple but effective strategy of getting through the day.

I am not sure how effective the actual "therapy" was for Connor. However, the psychologist started to really understand Connor and how his mind worked, what he found difficult and why he would either melt down or shut down in certain circumstances. With school life becoming more and more difficult, she offered to go into the school to talk to the teachers. As we were paying the bill, the school was more than happy to have a psychologist come and give a talk on autism to the teachers as part of their in-service training. I think it was only around 60–90 minutes for the talk and discussion. She would have happily covered a full day's course, but the time was not allocated and in many ways the bill would have been extortionate. It was an attempt to help educate the teachers about autistic spectrum disorders and most importantly about our son.

Connor was 10 years old when the relationship between him and the psychologist broke down. He was finding school very difficult and had had a particularly poor day, not that we knew it at the time. He did not want to go for his appointment and refused to go with her after school. His anxiety levels were through the roof. She was too firm. She spoke sternly to him at the school gate and he could not cope. I had both Stephen and Harry with me and Connor then heading into a full meltdown. What eventually transpired was that he ran away. Steve left work to search and we needed to call the police for help in finding him.

What we did learn was that he cannot be pushed into anything he does not want to do. This does not mean that we simply give in, we have strategies that we can use thanks to help in such situations. We will withdraw pressure to do something before a situation occurs. We use the concept of social stories to help prepare Connor, Stephen and Harry for anything that is out of routine or just getting back into a routine after a school holiday.

The breakdown of trust between Connor and the psychologist was devastating. We were left with no direct intervention to help him cope, give him strategies and ideas. At the time it felt as though we were back to square one. Of course, that wasn't the case, we had information and knowledge that we had not previously had.

More recently, Connor found himself in a difficult situation at school. If you ask him in an academic environment what is right and what is wrong, he can answer without problem. But faced with a situation where others are attempting to influence him, he can and did make the wrong choice. As a result, he asked to go and see the psychologist again. The trust was restored. She saw him and talked to him and helped him understand situations that he may be faced with again.

Child and Adolescent Mental Health Services

Our experience of the Child and Adolescent Mental Health Services (CAMHS) is rather mixed, from attending the most informative of courses for parents of children with autism, to simply not being able to get any form of help at the time we most needed it.

Connor was just six years old when we first sought help. Eighteen months later the community paediatrician made the referral to CAMHS for help with the management of Connor's behaviour, which was becoming more and more problematic. Just prior to his ninth birthday a further referral was sent as the first attempt had been declined because we as parents had not attended the "Early Bird Plus" programme. We were not told that the referral had been declined, nor were we told that any referral was subject to us attending a course on parenting our autistic son. We had been offered the course, but it coincided with my recovery from wrist surgery and I was unable to drive. Connor was almost nine and a half when we were informed that we were now at the top of the waiting list. A further three months passed before the appointment and visit to a clinical psychologist, not the child psychiatrist we had been referred to or had hoped to see. It was more than two years since that referral, since I sat in Dr Claisse's office almost in tears. A great deal had happened in that two-year period, much of it traumatic and challenging for us as parents and for Connor himself.

We talked to this clinical psychologist about the difficulties our son was having and had experienced at home and at school. It was evident from this appointment that the only "help" available to Connor was a form of cognitive behavioural therapy, an anxiety-management course. We were both reluctant as it would involve him being in a group situation, the very thing that he found the most difficult. Any direct intervention in the form of one-to-one appointments was simply not available. So that was it, take it or leave it. We had waited so long, what choice did we have?

Connor attended the course during school time. It lasted for around eight weeks, with a further session to follow up a few weeks later. It was a change of routine and he then had to adjust to going into school later in the day. Connor attended every week. He liked the biscuits, cake and juice on offer. He was not the only autistic child there, although the majority were neuro-typical. By the time we received a letter from one of the specialist clinical nurses who had conducted the course saying that Connor had overcome his fear of spiders, his fear of being on his own and his nightmares, we had sought emergency help from the CAMHS service. Connor had not shown or demonstrated at home or at school any prior fear of spiders or being on his own, nor had he experienced nightmares. He probably just said these on the course by copying the experiences of others. His challenging behaviour escalated after the course to the point that we became in crisis.

The emergency appointment with CAMHS eventually led to help from the child psychiatrist we had hoped to see nearly three years earlier. After a few appointments medication was offered to try to help Connor feel a little happier I think. It worked for a short period until the dosage was increased and then he felt awful. Any possible relationship or trust between the psychiatrist and Connor broke down and that was it. We continued with telephone appointments for a little while, but Connor refused to go and see her.

If I could turn back the clock and manage to convince the right people in the right places what Connor really needed, then perhaps things would have been different. We tried, we really tried. We have always felt that Connor needed some form of mentoring, a psychologist to listen to him, build up a bond with him, and understand him and how he sees the world. He went to see the private psychologist on a regular basis for a while, but he needed that something more. He has such a huge desire to form friendships and be social with others, he just finds it such a difficult thing to do.

It was when Stephen was referred to CAMHS for a cognitive assessment that we found the very person who would have been perfect for Connor. He was a young clinical psychologist with a manner that Connor would have taken to. As he sat there going through the cognitive assessment tests with Stephen on the two occasions that Stephen had to attend, I kept thinking, if only. He was so kind to Stephen. So precise in how he used language so that Stephen could understand and do his very best on the tests.

Our experience didn't change when we asked for help with Harry. This time it was just me who attended several appointments to talk about our youngest son. The clinical psychologist asked numerous questions and saw Harry in the CAMHS setting on only one occasion. At the end of a few sessions I asked whether they would be able to see Harry. The answer was the same as a few years earlier: the only options were for Harry to attend group sessions with other children, a course to cover emotional understanding, or one for anxiety management. I could not believe what I was hearing. Armed with experience on my side I asked the questions I should have asked for Connor. Was the course tailored specifically for autistic children? No. What academic evidence was there to show the results of such courses in autistic children? To their knowledge, no studies had been conducted. This time, we declined.

We continue to visit CAMHS for Harry's review appointments, around every six months, as Harry's paediatric care transferred to CAMHS when he was prescribed medication to help with anxiety. Something only a psychiatrist can prescribe, not a community paediatrician. Every time we walk in, the automatic doors make an awful squeaking noise. I have listened to this since our very first appointment, it is hideous. With three children on the autistic spectrum, all of whom have had appointments in this facility, on more than one occasion it has taken all my energy just to get them in the door. They are all so affected by sounds. So sensitive. I do so wish the NHS could simply fix that door.

The demands on the NHS's Child and Adolescent Mental Health Services have been in the news over the past months and years. It is such an important service despite our mixed experience. If only they had the resources to help Connor and Harry in a manner appropriate to their difficulties. If there had been early intervention in the form of psychology support for Connor, then would things have been different? Would he have been able to manage his primary school life better? Of course, there is no answer to the question. It is, however, an example of a child and his parents in desperate need of support and direct intervention, which were not available at the time they were most needed.

Befriending

It was around the time that Connor was being assessed for autism that a friend told me about a local charity that offered help to families with children that have additional support needs. It did not require input from CAMHS, reports or assessments, just a letter of referral from the head teacher or from a GP. Her three children all benefited from a befriending service that takes them out one afternoon after school every couple of weeks. It sounded perfect to help Connor. Off I went to the head teacher's office and asked for a referral. No problem at all, Connor was on the waiting list in no time.

As I said, it sounded perfect, and it was. There was obviously some time to wait as such a service would certainly be in demand. But Connor was eventually matched with the most wonderful of volunteers, Sophie. She was a student at St Andrews University, studying one of the sciences, I cannot quite remember which one. He was already showing an interest in all things science at this stage and it was the perfect match.

Not taking to many people, Connor took to Sophie so well. He was picked up in a taxi and dropped off again after the session. For a couple of days after each session he was so relaxed, it was therapy and actual direct intervention that we had so longed for. They walked around St Andrews, talked about everything and anything, ate chips, went to museums, and most of all they bought cheap Coke and Mentos and exploded them outside the charity's offices. Sophie wrote Connor the most wonderful of cards when she left university. There were a couple of other befrienders over the next couple of years, but no one could replace the wonderful Sophie and befriending sadly came to an end.

Harry is due to start soon. He has been on the waiting list for nearly two years. A massive increase in waiting time since Connor started, which demonstrates the pressure on any service to help families. I think it will be such a help to him. It is the most wonderful of charities and it helps people without the complexities of going through the "system" of referrals and reports before help can be given. The volunteers are just that though – they go through training before they can become a befriender, but they are not psychologists and it was when Connor's autism was all encompassing that the support they could provide was just not specialised enough.

Parent Awareness Programme for Autism Spectrum

The "Parent Awareness Programme for Autism Spectrum" was one of the most informative, interesting and enjoyable experiences that both Steve and I have attended. That sounds a little strange. It was a course aimed at parents with children on the autistic spectrum when the children were aged between 9 and 14 years. A course to inform and certainly not to judge. We were offered the course when Connor was finally seen by the child psychiatrist. There was a waiting list, naturally. We put our names down with no hurry to attend. After all, we had been through so much already, which meant that we were relatively well informed about autism by this stage, about our son, and the possibility of autism eventually being diagnosed in our other children.

Finally, by the time Connor was at secondary school and more settled, the letter came through that there was a place on a course for us. Amazingly, Steve's work diary meant that he could attend all the sessions. My diary meant that I would miss only one and that was for a paediatric appointment for Stephen.

We went along rather apprehensively to be greeted by two clinical psychologists who would be running the course. The lead psychologist was the very one who had just seen both Stephen and Harry for their autistic spectrum diagnostic pathway assessment. She was lovely, friendly and welcoming to everyone in the room. We all sat round, in couples mostly. Everyone nervous, what was going to happen, what would we be asked?

Like all courses, everyone had to introduce themselves and as we were all there as parents, we had to speak a little about our child. It was so obvious from this point that everyone had difficulties to cope with on a day-to-day basis. It was strangely relaxed.

The course covered so many aspects of living with an autistic child and coping with the various problems and behaviours that they present. Of course, no two children are the same, whether they are autistic or neuro-typical, but there were so many similarities and so many times when others in the room showed such empathy for their fellow parents. Everything said was confidential, so that is as much as I can say about other parents' situations. It was, however, relaxed, humorous at times, serious at other times. It was a forum where anything said was not judged but was discussed and provided a chance for parents to find solace in others.

During the course, for each of the areas covered we could identify the trait or difficulty in one or more of our children. When at home we often talk about the children, not referring to them by name but by number. That sounds awful, but it means that we can talk openly. They are not aware of what, or effectively who, we are talking about. One, two and three. Connor, Stephen and Harry. Without thinking, we adopted the same technique during the course, much to the amusement of the psychologists and the other parents. Somehow, it lightened what could otherwise have been difficult and emotional discussions.

We learned a great deal during the sessions. Even covering areas that we had already studied, for want of a better term, we gained more and more information during the eight weeks. Steve and I both agreed that we were sad when it came to an end. The more knowledge we have, the better decisions and actions we can take.

The one term for behaviour that we had not heard of before was "mind blindness". It was described as an inability to develop an awareness of what is in the mind of another person. Quite simply put, it would be the opposite of empathy. This does not mean that an autistic child cannot empathise with others, but it does relate to behaviours that Connor particularly will demonstrate when he is adamant that the answer he is getting is the wrong answer. Steve particularly refers to this when he is with Connor and he is being difficult. It has given us a much greater understanding of how his mind works, what is important to him and how we can help.

I had always thought that body language and facial imitation were the most difficult for Connor in situations where he is adamant about something but we are not in agreement. But perhaps it is more that he is unable to empathise with the answer or the point of view; he is effectively blind to our thoughts. There are similarities in Stephen. He certainly has times when he demonstrates mind blindness, he asks for things over and over again, despite us saying no repeatedly. However, it is not a trait of concern in Harry. Three autistic children, one, two and three as we referred to them, all different.

To finish the course, we had the privilege and pleasure to meet a young trainee clinical psychologist who was diagnosed on the autistic spectrum. I am not sure where he is based now, he was just about to submit his thesis at the time he came to speak to the parents on our course.

It was not something that I would ever have thought possible. A clinical psychologist with autism, Asperger's syndrome in this young man's case. As a psychologist you would meet people, and a lot of people – that is social interaction, however it is dressed up. How would an autistic person cope? He was truly amazing and both Steve and I thought that we were looking at the light at the end of a very long tunnel. He had spent so much of his youth trying to understand people, to understand the way their minds work, to understand what he should do. Effectively, he was studying the mind from such a young age that becoming a psychologist was an extension of simply trying to fit in. Still a young man, he has written a book titled *Raising Martians, From Crash-Landing to Leaving Home*.[7] It is a book about his experience and is aimed at how to help a child with Asperger's syndrome or high-functioning autism. It is a good read.

There are many courses available to help parents, carers, educators and all other people who come across autism in their lives. All I can say is that the "Parent Awareness Programme for Autism Spectrum" delivered by Fife CAMHS helped us enormously.

---

[7] Muggleton, J (2012) *Raising Martians, From Crash-Landing to Leaving Home*, London: Jessica Kingsley Publishers.

Chapter 6
THE BIG QUESTIONS

Nature versus nurture?

The final chapter of this book, but certainly not the final chapter for us as a family. There may be a number of questions that have come to mind as you have read through our story. For us there are four really big questions. What part does nature play in the nurturing process? What lessons can be learned from our experiences? What changes could be made to our future lives and the future of other children and families? Of course, the biggest question of all: where will the future take us?

As we embarked on the process to adopt, we envisaged what it would be like to be parents, how our children would grow up, what they might be interested in and what they would achieve in life. The issue of nature versus nurture did not form a significant part of the preparation course; in fact, I am struggling to recall it being discussed at all. There was plenty of information on how children come into the care system, and the types of background that they are likely to have come from, but little if nothing on how nature would play its part in the nurturing process.

While we were sitting in a café with the children aged around eight, six and four years, a fellow customer came over to our table to say what wonderful children, so well behaved, and "My, they do look like you both." Steve and I sat there smiling. The struggle to simply get them all seated, happy and behaving appropriately was one thing, to then be told that they look like us when clearly there are no genetics to support that, that was lovely for us. That acceptance from others that we are a family and a proper one.

So which has the greater influence, nature or nurture? There is, of course, no answer to the question, just observations and thoughts that support both. Our children certainly have picked up the way we speak. They are often mistaken for being English at school, robustly defending themselves saying that they were born in Scotland and are Scottish.

I looked out of the window at home a couple of years ago. There was Connor and his dad standing next to each other, contemplating what needed to be done in the garden. About the same height at that stage, they stood in the same pose, like two peas in a pod. But nature has certainly changed that. Connor is now significantly taller than Steve and he is only 13 years old. Still stands in the same pose, even more like his father now, clever, articulate and with such potential.

All our children are aware that they are adopted, we have always been open with them. We answer their questions to the best of our knowledge and ability as and when they arise. It is just part of how we came to be together. How we became a family. None of the boys has shown any interest in finding out anything detailed about their background, but they are still young and I am fully aware that they may want to pursue it when they are older. In many ways I hope that they are not interested, for me this is our family, no one else's. We have picked up the pieces of neglect, of trauma prior to birth, of diagnosed conditions that may be genetic, of difficult starts to their lives, and we are here, together and doing just fine.

They do have diagnosed conditions that may be genetic, autism for one. They do have conditions that come from their environment prior to birth, foetal alcohol syndrome and the possibility of drugs taken during pregnancy. Plenty of nature and experience to contribute to who they are. Like many adopted children, they also bring with them some life experience prior to being with us and part of our family. For Stephen, this included neglect and suffering. What effect that has had and will have on his development cannot be underestimated. So there are genetics and there are life experiences prior to adoption that will both contribute to who they are.

When we started the process to adopt, we both thought that nurture would play the much greater part in how our children develop and learn. I envisaged them following in my footsteps, being interested in sport and becoming competitive. I thought they would be golfers, certainly play golf at a young age. But that has not been the case at all – none is particularly interested in sport, although Stephen will sneak in late at night and suggest that he and Daddy cuddle up on the sofa and watch some sport. Just a good way of getting some time up late at night. I still hope that one or more of them will play golf at some stage, but I am not so sure. We are around halfway through getting them to adulthood and if I think about it now, with what we have dealt with and what is likely to come, nature has played a significant part in who they are. Much more of a part than I would ever have thought.

What we do as their parents is to attempt to provide an environment in which they can flourish. Now that sounds simple, but it is far from that. We help them deal with the effects of their conditions, whichever affects them as individuals. We continue to do our very best to provide them with guidance to get them through school life, to teach them about our values, of being kind to others, being polite, a sense of doing their best. Do our children have our values? Yes, I think they do, but in their own way. Genetics will always play its part.

There have been many studies on nature versus nurture. Adopted children are often compared to biological children in studies to try to ascertain the importance of one or the other on behavioural patterns. But then I often hear fellow mums in the playground say, "I would never have done that when I was young", or words to that effect. The environment itself is different from when we were young, and in many ways I see ourselves in our children, just not perhaps the parts I would have thought would come through the nurturing environment of our home. It is when we have new electronic equipment in the house, the children so quickly pick up how to work it. They become impatient with us for reading the instructions or taking our time. I remember vividly our first video recorder at home, my dad looking confused over the instructions and me taking over and wondering how on earth he couldn't understand it.

We love our children unconditionally. We are so proud of them and they continue to surprise us in what they can achieve. Only this week, Connor phoned me during his lunch break to say that he had passed his science exam with an A. He was so chuffed with himself. Tears came to my eyes, both from being proud and that he had phoned me to share the news. Sometimes it is hard, it is for all parents. We perhaps deal with more issues than many and not as much as others, but we continue to nurture and to guide our children, accepting that they are who they are, and some of that is unknown.

What lessons can be learned?

With what I know today, with what we have been through as a couple parenting our children, and if I could turn back the clock, would I still go through the adoption process? Yes, one hundred per cent yes. But that does not mean that lessons cannot be learned from what we have been through.

Like many prospective adopters, we just wanted a family. Our family. We were prepared for that not to be genetic but thoroughly believed that the nurturing process of bringing up our children would give us the family we longed for. And it has, just a family like no other. We have dealt with and continue to deal with the twin challenges of adoption and disability.

Reflecting on how we came to be together in the first place, lessons can certainly be learned from our experience. Embarking on the process to adopt is a huge decision and one that should not be taken lightly. There is and always will be pressure on prospective adopters during the assessment stage – the checks undertaken and references from others to show that the prospective adopters would be suitable parents are very hard indeed. In going through that process there must be honesty on both sides. By that, and in our case, I mean from the social work team assessing the applicants. There were many occasions during our assessment, and while waiting for a potential placement, that we were not kept informed, were not told everything that we should have been. We felt throughout that we were bending over backwards to do the right thing, to be available at the drop of a hat, to be accepted.

Particularly after being approved to adopt, a greater level of trust and respect would have made the wait for a child so much more bearable. There were lengthy visits requiring additional time off work, with no updates. It almost felt as though we were continuing to be assessed during the waiting process. The making of our family lay in the hands of these people and we would have welcomed a much more honest and open approach. From the cloak and dagger visit with details of our first son, to the social worker holding the paperwork and reading out salient parts, rather than us being allowed to read the report ourselves. And so importantly, the information that was held on files and not shared with us about potential conditions such as FAS and learning disabilities. We even found out during a visit to our GP, as she looked through Stephen's medical records, that there was a note about the suspected taking of drugs during pregnancy. I recall being specifically told that drugs had not been taken.

It is not that the information we should have received would have changed our decision. It is that it would have given us a greater level of knowledge to prepare for what might have been ahead. Similarly, we were not told about claiming child benefit, any adoption allowances or even payments for the purchase of necessary equipment. By the time we had Harry, our third son, we were eligible for an adoption allowance, and the adoption agency paid for a double buggy as we would now have two children still at that stage. Our financial stability was scrutinised as part of the assessment, but at no time were aspects of financial support or help discussed. It was only when Connor saw the private psychologist when he was 10 years old that we found out about allowances that were available for the boys because of their disabilities. When you have bought several pairs of shoes that were subsequently rejected because they no longer felt right, having disability living allowances certainly helps.

If I could turn back the clock, I would have asked more questions. Even at the very first stages in applying to adopt, during the preparation course, I would have asked more, gained as much information as possible to help us with what followed. A better understanding of the legal processes we would go through, what the chances were of adopting a child that would subsequently have additional support needs. The British Psychological Society[8] reports that "looked-after" children are four times more likely to require mental health interventions and nine times more likely to have special needs than those who grow up with their birth family. Does that correspond to children who are adopted? It certainly suggests that there is a much greater chance that adopted children will have some future difficulty or disability.

---

[8] Jackson S, McParlin P (2006) "*The Education of Children in Care*" The Psychologist 19, 2, 90–93.

When Connor was diagnosed as autistic, I thought I should advise social services as the condition could be genetic. I phoned the social work department and said that we had adopted our son five years previously and he had just been diagnosed with autism. I explained that I thought it would be information that might be relevant for them in the future. The person took the message and I heard nothing further – no one phoned back, no one has ever since looked for any further information on any of the children's development or progress. If there are other children from the same genetic background, then surely this is information that any prospective adopter would find useful in making their decision to adopt.

There are many academic articles that would suggest early diagnosis of conditions can help in providing the right support and environment for children to develop. Connor's autism was diagnosed when he was seven. I met his nursery teacher in the village shortly afterwards. She asked after him and I explained that he had been diagnosed as autistic. She commented that she had seen signs of this at nursery. There is clearly a need for early diagnosis to help both children and parents with what is to come next. Connor started nursery at the age of three and was there until the summer before his fifth birthday, which was between three and four years earlier than the actual diagnosis. Just maybe he would not have been expected to work in groups; part of his education might have been to interact socially and to learn the social signals required for inclusion. But this was missed by assuming that he should be able to act in an acceptable manner.

Children do not come with a manual, not even adopted children. In many ways it is nothing short of a miracle that we are where we are today. There have been numerous occasions where I have sat crying, with my head in my hands, not understanding where we were going wrong. The realisation and knowledge that we are not like other families, our problems and difficulties are different, and now being brave enough to embrace those differences.

What changes could be made?

In offering this account of our story, our experience in adopting and of parenting children with what are sometimes referred to as hidden disabilities, I hope to stimulate discussion, research and change to make the lives of our children and of other children better. It is only when we stand up and say what is happening that things can change. Things can be better for us and for others.

One of the questions I ask myself all the time is, how can a baby born with such a life-threatening condition, gastroschisis, then suffer from such awful neglect? How was Stephen left not being properly cared for in the first year of his life? He is certainly not alone. There are numerous reports in the media of failings in the care system resulting in tragic circumstances. Fortunately, Stephen's case did not result in such a situation. It was not a failure, he was taken into care, he was looked after in a stable foster home, but why did it take so long for him to be "rescued" from the situation? While it was not a failure, there must be lessons that can be learned from his circumstances. As his parents, we do not know much of what happened, it was all rather brushed under the carpet in discussion. I wish we had asked more questions, just so that we knew what to tell him later in life. The emphasis was on how he had developed in foster care and that he had some developmental delay. No suggestion of attachment disorder or any potential issues because of neglect.

Children with foetal alcohol syndrome have distinct facial features, such as small eyes, a thin upper lip and a smooth area between the nose and the lip. Looking back at the photographs of Harry at 11 months old, he had all these features. So why did it take so long for the possibility of FAS to be raised? Before a child is placed for adoption they undergo a medical assessment. There was no indication or suspicion of FAS in this report. It would not have changed our minds, but it would have given us time to research and understand the condition before symptoms such as ADHD and autistic-like behaviour presented themselves.

Reflecting on the adoption process itself, the preparation course and then the assessment stage, there was little emphasis on the challenges that might be ahead. It is not that this would have prevented us going forward to adopt, it is that we were not prepared for the types of challenges we have faced. We now know that looked-after children are more likely to have additional support needs, but what does this really mean? Looked-after children covers such a wide area, what about children who have been adopted? What research is there about the children who have been placed in permanent families? So many questions, so many unanswered questions. Informing social work services that our eldest son had been diagnosed autistic, there was no follow-up call, no further contact to enquire about his development or his difficulties. While I do not want our children to become statistics, it is so important that prospective adopters have all the information available to them, so that they can make the right decision.

Some conditions, such as attention deficit hyperactivity disorder, do not present until a child reaches a certain stage, for example around the age of six years for Stephen and Harry's ADHD symptoms. But there are suggestions that the chances of having a child with such difficulties are higher if the child is adopted. During the time when prospective adopters are waiting for a placement, there is not much happening, just waiting. Even written information, encouraging further research into conditions such as ADHD, autism and the like, would be useful. Surely information at this stage is better than "Your son has autism, here is your information pack."

Information is preparation for adoptive parents, not something that should or would prevent them from adopting. It is about having more knowledge to be able to deal with situations as they arise. To be able to identify what, if there is something, is wrong. Rather than putting everything down to the fact that the child is adopted, as we certainly did. Many adoptive parents, including us, look forward to the day that the legal proceedings are complete and there is no further involvement from social services, just wanting to be a normal family. But there may be times when help and support are needed and they should be available.

For Connor and for Harry, in care from birth, it was so clear from the information that was shared with us that adoption was the only sensible route. Why does it take so long? Connor was in care until he was 21 months old. That is nearly two years of his life in care. Coming from the circumstances that he did, surely that should not have been the case. Connor was with one foster carer, but for others that could mean being passed from foster carer to foster carer; the potential for attachment disorder and possible future mental health issues must be so enhanced. With Stephen, neglected, in care for 15 months and then placed for adoption at the age of two years three months, there is some evidence of attachment disorder. The circumstances of each adoptive case will be different. It is complicated. But there must be ways in which timescales can be reduced.

Our experience of education has certainly been mixed to date. Overall, it was the educational environment that Connor endured throughout his primary years that caused us some of the most difficult problems. Was mainstream education the best place for our son? Was it the right place? At times it was, but at other times it certainly was not. It took six years of primary school before he had any support at all. It was just a case of being sent to the head teacher's office when he could not be in the classroom, or worse still, barricading himself in the gym cupboard every afternoon.

It is our experience that many mainstream classes consist of multiple children with additional support needs. Children being taken out of class for reading or maths, coming back into the classroom, some with pupil support assistants to help, some without. On one occasion the school asked me to speak to a class about golf. It was not one of my children's classes, but I did know a few of the pupils. I put together a PowerPoint presentation, I linked the topic to maths, to science and, of course, to sport. During the hour I spent with the class, pupils went in and out; it was so disruptive, both to them and to the other children. That in itself would have caused my children to become stressed.

It was only when Connor headed off to secondary school that we saw a much more settled child. Being educated not in mainstream but in a nurturing classroom for children who also found it difficult to be in a mainstream environment. As you would imagine, the majority had an autistic spectrum diagnosis or autistic-like behaviour. If only such a class had been available for those seven years of primary education. A high school with an innovative and progressive idea that is seeing such success must be a model to look at for the future.

I often wonder about the psychological effects of mainstream education for children who would be so much more comfortable in a special class. A class that knows and understands their difficulties. Not having to fit in with the neuro-typical world, but fitting in in the autistic world to be educated and helped to develop. There are studies that suggest that social interaction should be with like-minded people in order to stimulate development, which means autistic people socialising or being in a setting with other autistic people. If that is the case, surely a more comfortable and accepting educational environment would ease the pressure on CAMHS? A rather political point that I should perhaps put out there for discussion and thought. It has certainly worked and is working for our son. It is one of the proudest things that has happened over the past few years, our son being at school and enjoying it. For our youngest son, we continue to battle. We continue to push for his education to be supported and adapted to his needs. It is certainly easier to say the right things, push at the right times, the second time around. Should that be the case? Should lessons have been learned and changes have been made? There have been some, but there could be so much more.

When that young psychologist with autism addressed the group on the "Parent Awareness Programme for Autism Spectrum" course, he spoke of the difficulties he had experienced in education. He spoke of the challenges that he faced as a young boy. He was in his mid-twenties. My eldest son was then 12 years old. There were so many similarities, so many situations that they had both gone through around 15 years apart. My question was simple: "What will it take to effect change for the better?"

Where will the future take us?

Leaving the courtroom on the day the Sheriff granted the adoption for our third son, we became a family of five. In three short years we went from a two, to a three, a four and then five. The Open Championship was at Turnberry in 2009, Harry had been placed with us just a few weeks earlier. I remember going with the children to stay with Steve, former colleagues walking past and waving, rather confused as the previous year we had had only one child. Such a quick change in circumstances. At that time, we had no idea what was to come.

Not only did adoption change our children's worlds, it changed ours, and so dramatically. We have faced more challenges than most, we have struggled, been extremely close to crisis, but we are somehow still here, and we continue to face the challenges presented to us. So much of this book talks about difficulties. There is, of course, so much more; those funny, proud, entertaining and enjoyable parts of parenting have and continue to be there for us. We celebrate the boys' achievements, just going to school happy and coming home the same after a good day is a massive achievement. Going on holiday is meticulously planned. We took the boys to Lanzarote and on the flights there and back we were complimented by passengers sitting near us on how well the boys behaved. How proud we were. If only they knew the extensive planning and social stories that went into making a journey a success. Having discovered that help is available to get the boys through airports, each of them has a lanyard to show that they have hidden disabilities. Less queueing and having the option to board a plane first, away from the hustle and bustle of other passengers, helps so much with making a journey more manageable.

I was once told for families coping with autism that family meals are only for The Waltons, for those of you who remember the iconic American series many years ago – all the family sitting round the dinner table, chatting and enjoying each other's company. Sometimes, just sometimes, we manage a family meal together and at the end Steve and I sit there with proud smiles on our faces. While other families may celebrate their child being player of the month in a particular sport, or achieving high awards at school or in a competitive environment, we are a family like no other. We are proud of those moments when our boys overcome something, for example Stephen managing to go into a shop where there are Halloween displays. For many years he could not go out for the weeks leading up to Halloween as it was simply too scary for him. Going to a new place, a museum, a swimming pool, and having an enjoyable experience. At their Granny's 80th birthday celebration, all the boys in a restaurant looking so smart in shirt and tie. Mind you, on the way Harry announced that he looked like the children from Buckingham Palace and he didn't like it. It was so hard not to laugh.

At this moment in time we have two children still in primary school and our eldest son in secondary school. We have challenges that we are dealing with, and every day presents a new scenario that we manage and hopefully overcome. It is not easy by any means.

I sometimes look back at photographs of when we first had the boys, from those times of slides, paddling pools and splash mats, the boys holding baby lambs at our friends' farm. They are our boys, one hundred per cent our boys. They have different genetics, they have their own natures that so contribute to who they are, but we provide them with an environment in which we hope they will flourish.

It is when we let our guard down that many of the problems have occurred. When we think we are doing fine is when we forget to prepare, we forget to tell those social stories of what is going to happen, what is coming next. It is when we forget to look out for signs of sensory overload that we then handle meltdowns and heightened emotions.

The question is, where will the future take us? That, of course, is unknown for anyone. I feel a little like we may be in the calm before the storm at present. All parents talk of those teenage years and we will be parenting three teenagers with disabilities. How will their disabilities affect how they will be through that physical change of adolescence? I just do not know. What I do know is that there is a great deal of information out there to help prepare us, information through autism and adoption charities, through Facebook groups such as the Autism Discussion Page,[9] and many others. We will continue to look for knowledge and information to help and in some ways to comfort us as we deal with issues.

Will the boys all be able to live independently? That is such a huge consideration for us going forward. I think that both Connor and Harry probably will. But for Stephen, that is so much more unknown. I often ask the boys what they would like to be when they grow up, it is one of those questions that all adults seem to ask children. Connor is approaching the stage where he is being asked a similar question at school, when he is choosing subjects to study. He is heading towards something mechanical or in the engineering field. I just hope that he can continue to cope with education, to enjoy school or college in the future. I do worry about him, in his words he is "controlling his autism", trying to fit in and be part of mainstream education. Harry, well, who knows. One minute he would like to be a fighter pilot, the next he realises that is a little dangerous and perhaps something less so would be better. Stephen, at eleven-and-a-half years old, severely dyslexic and struggling to read anything, learning disabled with ADHD and autism, he would like to be a palaeontologist. That is, of course, when he is not a superhero or a dinosaur. I am simply proud of him for knowing what a palaeontologist does. He does get so excited when David Attenborough comes on the television, his favourite presenter of all time, closely followed by Dr Brian Cox.

---

[9] Nason W (2014) *The Autism Discussion Page on the Core Challenges of Autism*, London: Jessica Kingsley Publishers.

One day we will be a couple again. Children grow up and become adults. In many ways they grow too quickly and in others I look forward to that freedom again. The chance to just get up and do something that is not planned, something on a whim. It may be simply going out for lunch or heading off to a show or concert, playing golf, something unexpected, something "normal". We are a family that has come together through adoption and through disability. I am so proud of us all and everything we have achieved.

BIBLIOGRAPHY

Adoption UK (2017) Living with Foetal Alcohol Spectrum Disorders (FASD). Available at www.adoptionuk.org/resources/article/living-foetal-alcohol-spectrum-disorders-fasd, accessed 30 January 2018.

BBC (2017) "Chris Packham: Asperger's and Me." Available at www.bbc.co.uk/programmes.

BBC Radio 4 (2017) File on 4, "Adoption: Families in Crisis." Available at bbc.co.uk/programmes.

Doherty K, McNally P, Sherrard E (2000) *I Have Autism… What's That?* London: National Autistic Society.

Jackson S, McParlin P (2006) "The Education of Children in Care", *The Psychologist*, 19, 2, 90–93.

Muggleton J (2012) *Raising Martians, From Crash-Landing to Leaving Home*, London: Jessica Kingsley Publishers.

Nason W (2014) *The Autism Discussion Page on the Core Challenges of Autism*, London: Jessica Kingsley Publishers.

NHS (National Health Service) (2016) Autism Spectrum Disorder. Available at www.nhs.uk/conditions/autism/, accessed 30 January 2018.

NHS (National Health Service) (2016) Attention deficit hyperactivity disorder. Available at www.nhs.uk/conditions/attention-deficit-hyperactivity-disorder-adhd/, accessed 30 January 2018.

NHS (National Health Service) (2017) Foetal alcohol syndrome. Available at www.nhs.uk/conditions/foetal-alcohol-syndrome/, accessed 30 January 2018.

INDEX